Illustrated

SHELBY

BUYER'S ★ GUIDE™

Jay Lamm and Nick Nicaise

Motorbooks International
Publishers & Wholesalers

To Alberta and Nancy

First published in 1992 by Motorbooks International Publishers & Wholesalers, PO Box 2, 729 Prospect Avenue, Osceola, WI 54020 USA

© Jay Lamm, 1992

The information in this book is true and complete to the best of our knowledge. All recommendations are made without any guarantee on the part of the author or Publisher, who also disclaim any liability incurred in connection with the use of this data or specific details

We recognize that some words, model names and designations, for example, mentioned herein are the property of the trademark holder. We use them for identification purposes only. This is not an official publication

Motorbooks International books are also available at discounts in bulk quantity for industrial or sales-promotional use. For details write to Special Sales Manager at the Publisher's address

Library of Congress Cataloging-in-Publication Data
Lamm, Jay William.
   Illustrated Shelby buyer's guide / Jay Lamm, Nick Nicaise.
       p.   cm.—(Motorbooks international illustrated buyer's guide series)
   Includes index.
   ISBN 0-87938-604-5
   1. Shelby automobile—Purchasing.
   I. Nick Nicaise.   II. Title.   III. Series.
TL215.S48L36   1992
629.222′2—dc20   91-42331

On the front cover: *The 289 Cobra (foreground) was the tenth Cobra built with the 289 engine. Owner Lynn Park has raced it in vintage races for more than a decade. The 1965 GT350 (background) remains in the hands of original owner Jim Schield, who bought the car in 1965 and has raced it ever since, first in slalom competitions and more recently in vintage races.* Jerry Heasley

On the back cover: *A 1969 Shelby Mustang GT500 convertible with the 428 Cobra Jet engine, and a GT40 Mk IV, which was a winner at both Sebring and Le Mans.* Nick Nicaise

Printed and bound in the United States of America

Contents

Acknowledgments

We would like to thank the following people and organizations for their assistance in preparing this book:

Dave Brownell, Tony Cervone, Chrysler Motor Corporation, Classic Roadsters, Brian Codjikari, Contemporary Classics Motor Car Company, Dodge Division of Chrysler, Michael Dregni, ERA Replica Automobiles, Mike Farber, Ford Motor Company, Michael Fry, Elizabeth Gardiner, Bob Hall, Budd Hickey, Ellen Houston, Cathy Kastriner, Rick Kopec, Mary LaBarre, LAExotics, Mike Lamm, Robert Lamm, Lamm-Morada Publishing, Vincent Liska, David P. Matthews, Moss Motors, Nancy Nicaise, Brett O'Brien, Howard Pardee, Mark Rhoades, John Richotte, Edward W. Scudder, Shelby American Automobile Club, Shelby Automotive, Inc., Shelby Dodge Automobile Club, Sports Car Club of America, Rich Taylor, C. Van Tune, Doug Waschenko, Wallace A. Wyss.

Introduction

It all boils down to a number of "happy" circumstances. Carroll Shelby had gone from Texas obscurity to the winner's circle at Le Mans by the time heart troubles forced him from the driver's seat in the early 1960s.

Where would he go from there? Well, Carroll Shelby started new careers the way other people start crossword puzzles, and the job he wanted most was building world-beating race cars. The most logical route was to go hybrid: stuff an American V-8 into a responsive sports chassis and try to capture the best of both worlds. Allard, Cunningham and Facel-Vega had made it work to some degree in the 1950s, but there were hundreds of others that didn't get as far. Until Shelby came along, hybrids had never quite gone all the way on the track or the dealer's lot.

Shelby's car would be different. It would be the only hybrid in history to achieve a real pedigree—a thoroughbred mongrel, if you like. Shelby's true genius was not as a designer, an engineer, or even a driver; it was as a manager of affairs. His unique skill lay in finding the right people, making the right decisions, seizing the right opportunities, setting the right inspiration, and always delivering on his promises. In a complex and often cutthroat business, Carroll Shelby was (and is) a man to be trusted. Nothing less would do.

In the end, it's Shelby himself who makes these cars so special. Like Colin Chapman or Enzo Ferrari, Carroll Shelby has put a bit of his own personality into every car that bears his name. You're not just buying four wheels and a gob of horsepower, you're buying a part of the legend.

Investment Ratings

The *Illustrated Buyer's Guide* series from Motorbooks has long relied on a simple investment or collectibility rating system to indicate which cars of a given marque seemed most likely to appreciate over time. For this book, however, the usual five-star investment ratings have been replaced with a new system, a 1-10 scale of desirability that indicates not so much investment potential as how badly a collector's *gotta have it*. (And, because we're dealing with the cars from Carroll Shelby here, you'll find that this book contains a few elevens.)

The reason's pretty simple. First and most importantly, as of the early 1990s, investment automobiles have appreciated so strongly that predicting what will come next is almost impossible, and it misses the point of automobile collecting.

From the healthy sums they now command, high-dollar collectibles like Cobras may appreciate in the future or—like Ferraris and many other exotics—level off and even decline in value. The only responsible advice one can give in today's market is that a buyer should purchase a car for the very simple reason that he or she *wants to own it*. That way, while you might be pleasantly surprised later, you'll never be disappointed. Don't buy one to make a pile of dough, buy it because *you've gotta have it*.

The second reason for this new system is that almost *all* Ford-powered Shelbys qualify as five-star collectibles by anyone's standards; to call a 289 Cobra or GT40 anything less is ludicrous. But then what does that make the even more collectible Daytona or Mark IV?

For this book, a rating of ten is the highest you can get; and then there are the elevens. Anyone who has experienced these cars up close will understand.

260 and 289 Cobra

A Bit of Background

Carroll Shelby originally wanted Chevrolet to supply the engine for his still-hypothetical sports car. But the boys from Warren, Michigan, couldn't oblige; they already had a V-8 powered sports car, thank you, and it was doing just fine. They would live to regret that decision.

Ford, on the other hand, was quite happy to help out, in part because Shelby's timing was excellent. The Ford Motor Company was phasing out its old Y-block V-8 and phasing in a new generation of lightweight engines they were eager to brag about. They sent Shelby a couple of 221ci (cubic inch) V-8s to play with, and he came away impressed. The light-blue lumps from Dearborn ran just fine; now the question was, what to *do* with them?

Over lunch one day with some buddies from *Sports Car Graphic*, Shelby's answer fell

With its mild early flares and wire wheels, the original Cobra boasted tremendously clean lines. Later scoops and flares added muscle, but it's up to buyers to decide which style they like better; it shouldn't affect the cost much either way. *Nick Nicaise*

from the sky. AC Cars Limited, the gracious sports car manufacturer of Thames Ditton, England, was in trouble.

They'd been winning races like mad with a hot little number called the AC Bristol, a tidy car with some interesting history. The Bristol started out as the AC Ace, a production sports car derived from a one-off racer built by John Tojiero; that car's classic styling was, in turn, derived from Ferrari's early 1950s 166MM Barchetta. Dropping in a Bristol engine—and *that* was a direct copy of an earlier BMW mill—in 1956 gave them a car that won a lot of races and kept the company afloat. The AC Bristol used transverse-leaf-spring suspension at both ends, a tube frame, and a lightweight aluminum body. There was nothing revolutionary about it, and in fact nothing particularly modern. Still, it was quick and nimble enough to virtually own E-Production racing in its heyday.

Factory Weber setup with dedicated Cobra intake manifold is one of the nicest-looking engine packages around. Not really suitable for the street, on the track this package was a killer. Synchronizing and tuning all four carburetors is a highly skilled operation. *Nick Nicaise*

All the racing and go-fast goodies on this 289 add up to a valuable piece. Of course, it's not so much the equipment as the *history* of that equipment that really determines the value. Accessories cost money, but to a show-minded collector each one lowers the car's value by exactly the cost of removing it. Among the rarest Cobra add-ons is an aerodynamic hardtop used by AC at Le Mans but abandoned shortly thereafter. The hardtop alone is worth a tremendous amount of money, but don't bet on finding one. *Nick Nicaise*

Aluminum-grid grille inserts on 289 Cobras are easy to damage and a pain to repair, and a nice, straight example like this is one of the first things to look for. Once a Cobra has been hit and repaired, often you can't get the grille in the nose again. *Nick Nicaise*

But the word had now come down that Bristol was ceasing production of the engine, and that left AC high and dry. Despite its age, tangled roots, and dated suspension, the Bristol was a fine sports car. Its passing, the lunch guests commiserated, would be mourned. "Or would it?" mused Shelby.

At the same time, Ford was declaring an imminent displacement bump of its 221 up to 260ci, and that was the last part of the puzzle. Here was AC in need of an engine, and Ford improving what was already a great one—Shelby couldn't have asked for a better combination. He packed his bags and headed for England, via Detroit.

On the basis of his past accomplishments and his Texas charm, he secured an experimental 260 V-8 from Ford and a chassis from AC. It foreshadowed the organizational wizardry that would lead to the most awesome cars of the 1960s. Shelby could have written a book: *How to Start a Sports Car Company with No Money Down.*

At Thames Ditton, AC started putting the pieces together. The Ford engine and a Borg-Warner four-speed slotted into the small car like a dream. What didn't come so easily was getting the rest of the components to handle the massive torque of the V-8, something AC's designers never planned on when they started the design of the Ace. After shredding

CSX2473, the 1968 B-Production champion and a long-time contender in SCCA Production racing. Its history firmly established, CSX2473 is one of the most valuable leaf-spring Cobras around, but it's just too much fun to leave in the garage. One of the greatest things about Cobras is the way that owners still use them. *Nick Nicaise*

Can't scrape together enough petty cash for a Cobra? Well, there's always the 260/289 Sunbeam Tiger, developed by Carroll Shelby for the Rootes Group. The Tiger never had the brakes or the balance of a Cobra, but for folks with real-world pocketbooks it's always been a contender. *Nick Nicaise*

a good number of the original AC pieces and having them replaced with beefier parts, the hybrid monster was ready for testing.

It was early 1962 when Shelby muscled the first soon-to-be Cobra around the Silverstone circuit in England. When he was done, he knew what he had produced still needed work, but also knew that it would stomp a Corvette—his car's natural enemy on the street and in Sports Car Club of America (SCCA) production racing—into gravy even as it sat.

Shelby took the tale of his Anglo-American hybrid back to Detroit and sold Ford on the project. In a brilliant move that must have seemed crazy at the time, Ford agreed to supply Shelby with engines and running gear in exchange for a small "Powered by Ford" plaque on the fender.

Their backs against the wall with the cancellation of the Bristol engine, AC was even more generous. They agreed to build chassis and bodies to Shelby's specs, then ship them to California *on credit*. The only proviso was that the AC badge remain on the car. Now all Shelby had to do was develop, market, organize, publicize, campaign, and construct his own cars, company, and racing team. Easy!

The Cobra Comes Alive

The day the first bare AC chassis arrived in Los Angeles was the day that Shelby trucked it to Dean Moon's speed shop in Santa Fe

As the 289 aged, wider flares appeared around CSX2160 to cover wire wheels up from 5.5In to 6in even. All wire wheels should be checked every few weeks by lightly tapping on each spoke with a screwdriver; a ringing means the spoke is sound, a dull thud means it needs replacement. Bad spokes can be deadly. *Nick Nicaise*

Cobra Numerology

Cobras were all assigned a relatively simple VIN (vehicle identification number) consisting of CSX (Carroll Shelby Experimental, though the X stood for Export on the CSX2000) and a four-digit number. The first digit denotes the vehicle type: CSX2– is a leaf-spring, small-block car, while CSX3– would be a coil-spring big-block. The other three numbers are a *rough* indication of the car's job number. (For example, CSX2115 may well have been finished before CSX2111.)

The rare car designated simply CS was built for racing by AC's own stable or a close confederate; COB cars were built for the British market, and COX designates an export model not intended for the United States.

Leaf-spring cars have the full VIN or the second, third and fourth digits in the following places:
- The chassis bracket between the steering box and fuel pump on worm-and-sector equipped cars, and the passenger's A-arm bracket on cars fit with rack-and-pinion steering. (Full VIN.)
- Hood and trunk latch with panel raised and latch locked.
- Handwritten by engraver on reverse of trunk-cockpit dividing panel.
- Handwritten by engraver on underside of transmission tunnel.
- Stamped on top of door hinge behind leather cover flap.
- Cars after CSX2200 also have an AC Cars ID plate with chassis and engine number included on the passenger's side footbox.

Coil-spring cars use the same locations except for the main underhood number, which is stamped into the passenger's shock tower above the spring carrier.

The most important thing to do the first time you lay your eyes on a potential buyer Cobra is to check all the serial numbers and see that they're in place and matching. Bring a flashlight, a soft toothbrush (to wipe away grime covering numbers), and a dental mirror to look into tight spots.

On leaf-spring cars from CSX2200 on, there are two stampings on the AC Cars ID plate: the top one refers to the chassis number and the bottom refers to the engine block number, which is also listed on a boss over the front driver's side spark plug. The engine code will match between block and plate if everything's on the up and up.

The chassis and engine ID plate numbers should be stamped in two slightly different sizes, and the numbers invariably don't line up too well. If the plate has two clean, even, and matched sets of numbers, it's a reproduction tag and you have to ask yourself why.

The standard street Cobra gauge layout was simple and reasonable. Stewart-Warner gauges (left, with angled bezels) appeared when Shelby realized they were cheaper and more reliable than the original Smiths units (right, with rounded bezels). Proper Smiths gauges in good condition are exceedingly hard to come by, so look for sound units already on the car. *Nick Nicaise*

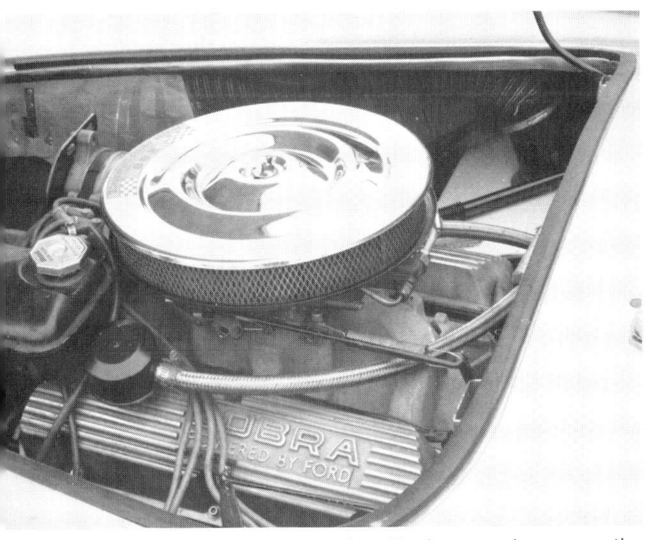

Most people are surprised by how unglamorous the basic Cobra engine looks in its natural state. Dowdy Ford pancake air cleaner doesn't help, but a sharp eye notices the impressively high intake manifold— that's not your standard cooking Mustang piece. *Mike Lamm*

A little ingenuity—two zip ties—should keep this genuine AC racing cap from flying open at speed. This owner has resisted the temptation to go to a larger Shelby quick-fill unit, and has preserved a little piece of history in the process. *Mike Lamm*

Springs and slotted in the Ford V-8 engine. The car was designated CSX2000, the CSX standing for Carroll Shelby Export on this car *only*, and the two-series serial number denoting its leaf-spring suspension.

For CSX2000, the engine was a 260 that Ford had hopped up in its own skunk works with solid lifters, a Holley four-barrel, and bumped compression. By the very same evening it was in the car and Shelby and Dean Moon were out looking for victims.

What they were driving was a hybrid hot rod; there were plenty of those running around southern California, and none of them had become production cars or world-beating racers. What Shelby needed was money, publicity, and a talent pool to push the car beyond one-off status. His talents in those areas are really what made the Cobra possible; his ability to pursue the project beyond its early stages, and to convince all the right people that his hot rod was better than everyone else's. It would be trust and money, in equal and large doses, that would make Shelby's company run.

A watershed in his efforts came when Dave Evans, one of Shelby's key accomplices at Ford, invited Carroll to show his car on the Ford stand at the New York Auto Show. Decked out in blinding yellow paint, the little AC—still a basically unheard of and unknown quantity—generated enough excitement to persuade not just Ford but also a fistful of dealers to jump on the bandwagon.

Next he needed hard cash, and to get that he needed exposure. Shelby deftly parlayed his back-slapping relationship with most of America's automotive journalists into full-color magazine covers and articles. As good at public relations as he was with the Le Mans-winning Aston Martins, he threw coat after coat of different-colored paint onto the same prototype sports car. To magazine readers, it seemed like Shelby's cars were already falling off the production line; in reality, hot-shoe magazine writers were flogging the living daylights out of the one and only Cobra in the world. Lord help Shelby if one of them had stacked it up.

With everything finally lined up but the cars themselves, Shelby's going concern moved to Venice, California, and into the premises recently vacated by Lance Reventlow's Scarab operation. Phil Remington, one of the Scarab's main players, came along for the ride, and proved instrumental in Cobra development. The third car that came to Venice from Thames Ditton, CSX2002, received the second hopped-up Ford 260 and became the first Cobra racer. Racing, of course, was what this project would be all about.

From those beginnings came every Carroll Shelby creation afterward, if not as a direct descendant of the AC-Ford hardware, then from the fame and good will that Shelby generated with his first efforts. The small-block AC Cobra is certainly not the most expensive Shelby vehicle in this book—nor, by a longshot, the cheapest—but it's considered by many to be the best. Shelby, Remington, and the rest of the crew took a sports car that was by then quite old, with a suspension that looked downright lame on paper, slotted in an engine that was never meant for it, and came up with the fastest thing you could drive on the street—or the track.

The Cobra in Production

It often seems that no two small-block Cobras are exactly alike, though many of them reflect a logical progression of equipment and evolution. Though the Cobra was at first considered little more than a hot rod—even after its performance on the track proved its sophistication under the skin—it was in fact a pretty well thought out machine. Considerable reengineering went into the very first car that AC put together, and the car received constant production-line changes as the needs arose. If a component broke on a Shelby on Sunday, chances were a revised part would be well on the way to production by Monday.

That led to constant changes and updates, which makes it difficult to pin down the exact equipment a given Cobra should have. It's important, however, to determine as accurately as possible how much of a given car is correct "as delivered." This not only ensures that the car will be a good investment—an original Cobra is *generally* but not *always* worth more than one that's been modified—but it's also a good way to know you've got a solid, strong automobile on your hands.

For better or worse, nonfactory modifications will lower the value of an individual car

A variety of throttle linkages had to be worked up to fit all the intake applications of the Cobra. The actual format is not really as important as the soundness of the engineering; solid joints and mounting points like these are not always found on cars that have been modified after they left Shelby American. *Mike Lamm*

Here's why so many Cobras lost their original expansion tanks to chromed aftermarket replacements; a plain-Jane black bucket at the front of the engine just doesn't look that good. Still, if you want authenticity, that's the part you ought to have. *Mike Lamm*

Cobra Chassis and Body Integrity

You'd think that an aluminum car like the Cobra would eliminate the need to worry about rust. Not so. Sure, the Cobra's body and inner panels were aluminum, but the frame rails and the tubing that support the bodywork were steel, and wholly susceptible to rot.

Cobras that have seen duty in a Midwest winter (which, of course, means relatively few of them) can experience serious and dangerous amounts of frame rust. The most vulnerable spot is the driver's side mainframe rail; water can enter through the holes drilled to secure the brake-line clips and eat away at the car from the inside. Every piece of the frame and support tubing, however, needs to be looked at with a sharp eye before buying.

The frame rails of a Cobra can also be tweaked out of alignment by an accident or even the stress of a hard bump. Look under the car for obvious bending and twisting, and if that test is successful, take the car to a trustworthy frame expert and have him check it out as well. While the car is up in the air, go along the frame rails with a magnet looking for body filler. A serious bang in the frame that's been filled and painted over may be hiding a dangerous weak spot in the car.

Aside from rust in the traditional sense, Cobras are also prey to the more insidious demon of electrolysis. When two dissimilar metals like aluminum and steel come into contact, electrons travel between them and eat away the structure of both. On a geologic time scale this happens almost immediately, but in our lifetimes it's nothing to worry about—unless moisture (particularly salty moisture) is introduced between the metals. When this happens, the process is sped up considerably and can start to eat away at a Cobra's heart.

The most common place for electrolytic corrosion to occur on a Cobra—aside from the battery area, of course—is where the aluminum body hooks around the frame tubes and supports, especially right behind the wheels. Trouble here usually is visible as bubbling and holes in the aluminum itself, but an unscrupulous restorer can patch this up quite easily. Look closely for fisheyes and other signs of tampering all along the bottom of the car's body. Body and chassis corrosion are the most expensive ills to which the Cobra can fall prey.

The 289s set up for serious racing received not only an oil cooler ahead of the radiator but also an additional scoop in the bodywork to bring in air. The scoop essentially makes this car impractical for anything but track use—it's low enough to snag on all sorts of street obstacles. *Mike Lamm*

Already more of a romantic add-on than a realistic accessory, headlight stone guards are a quite acceptable period addition to any Cobra. Road racing and hillclimb cars did, in fact, have good use for them. *Mike Lamm*

The aerodynamic fastback roof of the first Le Mans Cobras necessitated cutting the trunk in half and fitting new hinges to the bottom. Just one more thing that makes these cars unique and valuable. *Mike Lamm*

unless they're proven to be part and parcel of a historic vehicle's race configuration, or unless the resale value of the added parts outweighs the cost of restoring the vehicle back to original specifications.

To make things even more confusing for the buyer looking for an as-delivered car, a fair number of the earliest Cobras and a few handfuls of the later ones weren't built in Shelby's California digs at all, they were finished off to Shelby's specs by Ed Hugas' dealership in Pittsburgh. It's even possible that a few were put together by another dealer in Rhode Island. All this considered, a buyer can only find solace in the fact that if he (or she) does his homework correctly and judges a car fairly, the next buyer ought to evaluate the car in pretty much the same way.

Fortunately, though, verifying the things that really matter turns out to be easier than one might expect. That's due in no small part to the exhaustive work of the Shelby Amer-ican Automobile Club (SAAC), which has cut through the myths and lore of the Cobra story and found the hard facts. Their assistance will be invaluable when it comes time to buy, and to get their undivided attention it's a good idea to join the club beforehand.

The one large monkey wrench that still gets thrown into the works is when you're dealing with a car built originally for Shelby's own or a serious privateer's racing use. Many of these featured innovations and additions that only showed up on the production cars much later. (Such a car's history, of course, is still likely to be documented with the SAAC.)

In any case, after the first couple of hundred cars, things settled down and the specifications start to make a lot more sense. In the beginning, all Cobras featured 260ci V-8s, worm-and-sector steering, Lucas electrical systems, no side vents, and Smiths gauges (which have become real bears to find in good shape today). Real leather upholstery, 12in Girling disc brakes, full top and side curtains, and real knockoff wheels were all part of the package, while cars could be ordered in red, maroon, dark and pure blue, silver, black, and white. The original price of admission was just a tad under six grand.

After the first seventy cars, the stock rear-axle ratio changed from 3.54:1 to 3.77:1 (European cars stayed with the 3.54, though) and a Ford generator replaced the Lucas unit. After seventy-five cars, the 260ci engine was swapped for the 289. CSX2126 brought rack-and-pinion steering and a dished steering wheel; early flat wheels are hard to come by, while later dished wheels are made in repro form, and repro wheel centers are available but they're not great. It's best to stick with the original if you can find it. Steering racks are also much easier to locate and repair than worm-and-sector boxes.

With CSX2160, slightly wider fender flares appeared accompanied by seventy-two-spoke, 6.0in wire wheels (up from 5.5in) and side vents. CSX2188 ushered in a self-adjusting handbrake. With the 200th car off the line, Ford electronics and Stewart-Warner gauges (these gauges are available in decent but not great repro form) replaced the Lucas and Smiths components, and a Ford alternator replaced the earlier Ford generator (easy-to-find junkyard pieces).

Both Shelby American and individual owners engaged in some retrofitting of newer parts to older cars; for Shelby American, at least, this was limited strictly to competition cars and to special requests by private owners. (Shelby American never made an effort to retrofit new hardware to already-constructed Cobras unless the current owner was willing to pay for it.) They did, however, constantly update their own stable of competition cars: All of the factory's 260 racing cars, for example, were updated to 289s during their careers. Private owners'

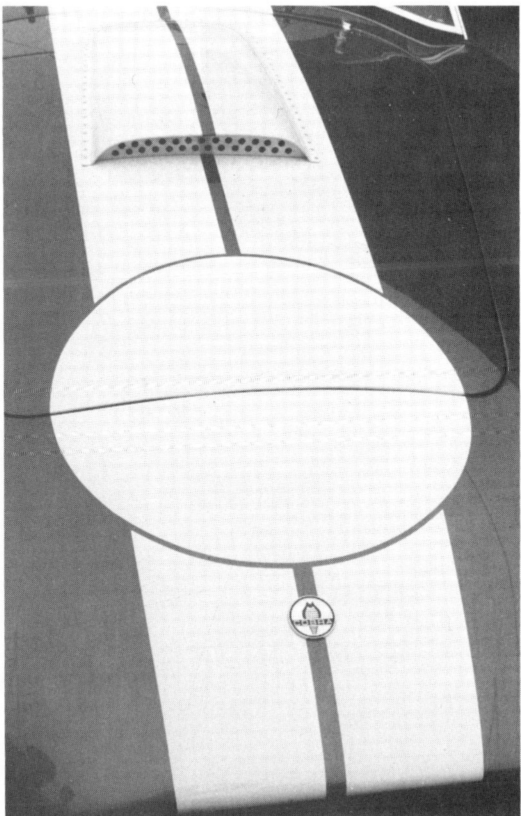

Baffled hood scoop intake prevents rocks and assorted crud from entering the intake system. This is something you shouldn't see on a Cobra unless it has an interesting racing history; Nassau, rallies, and hillclimbs usually precipitated it. *Mike Lamm*

Large, low side vents of the Le Mans Cobras and replicas led the way to the higher, smaller vents on all Cobras after CSX2150. Vents like these indicate a history worth telling. *Mike Lamm*

A great variety of hood scoops will be found as one looks over a number of Cobras. Most are legitimate performance additions, like this riveted Le Mans piece installed by AC. Others are an aftermarket hash, but such a dizzying array of factory installations occurred that a buyer's own taste will have to be the best judge of a scoop's value. *Mike Lamm*

modifications are much harder to track, of course, but it's a safe bet that many street 260s received the same engine-swapping treatment.

Added to the running changes were a dizzying array of options, both factory- and dealer-installed, which could personalize each Cobra. The options fell into basically two categories—cosmetic and performance. The most common cosmetic options were in chrome: exhaust tips, bumper and grille guards, chrome wire wheels, luggage rack, outside mirror, and tuned air cleaner. The others included wind wings, a Smiths interior heater, AM radio and antenna, whitewall tires, plastic sun visors, a Ford C-4 automatic transmission (about thirty were produced), and a removable hardtop.

The list of performance options was understandably longer. Just scratching the surface on the suspension, steering and brake side were: front and rear antiroll bars, Koni adjustable shocks, stiff front and rear springs, chromed wire wheels, competition alloy wheels (fender flares came with the alloys), a steering brace, alloy brake calipers, front and

FIA and USRRC Cobras were a fantastic combination of engineering and simplicity. It's no wonder that they're usually second only to the Daytonas in value. *Nick Nicaise*

rear brake scoops, and a twin master cylinder conversion kit.

Engine options covered considerable ground above and beyond the street-competition reworking of heads and entire powerplants that were available from the factory. The induction system alone was offered with one four-barrel carburetor (common), two four-barrels (rare), four twin-choke Webers (somewhere in between) or a 3x2 intake manifold (never actually made). Hot cams, pistons, rods, crank, and a two-coil Spalding Flamethrower ignition system never hurt anything, and why not throw in the tuned Nassau exhaust headers and side pipes while you were at it?

Though the cooling system on even the first Cobra was never as bad as its reputation, you could upgrade it with an alloy Harrison crossflow unit (as used on the 1962 Corvette) anyway, and throw in an oil and differential cooler kit to boot. The large-capacity Aviad oil sump might not be a bad idea, either. A hood scoop and cold-air box came standard with the Weber kits, but a variety of different setups found their way onto most any car.

Simply put, there is no one "correct" mechanical specification for a Cobra on the basis of its production number. Think instead about whether the equipment included with a given car is appropriate for its time period and, more important, whether or not it all *works right.*

A large competition-type fuel filler was handy if you optioned the car with the aluminum 37gal fuel tank, and competition lights,

With historical basis, the unique rear flares, side vents, and hood scoop on this car are valuable; without documentation, though, they would simply be things that would cost money to set right. Cobras are some of the most-modified cars of all time, but originality is definitely becoming important again. *Nick Nicaise*

Plated expansion tank and braided hoses are traditional speed shop pieces that have found their way onto a lot of Cobras. They're easy to replace if desired, but most owners wouldn't bother. The quad Weber setup, on the other hand, is something most everyone would pay extra for, although drivability suffers compared to a simpler setup.

Original Pieces

Over the last ten years or so many Cobras have been extensively rebuilt and brought to as-new condition by their owners. While this is a good thing for preserving the marque, in another way it's creating a problem.

It means that fewer and fewer Cobras are sporting lots of tatty but genuine pieces from the factory. That's bad for the history of these cars and perhaps tough on fans emotionally, but only recently has it become an issue financially. Today, many buyers are more interested in having, say, a scuffed but original AC wheel center than a reproduction piece, or a genuine, beat-up egg-crate grille rather than a pristine copy. Original seatbelts, paint, and leather in presentable condition may well be more valuable than modern replacements, and to my mind, at least, they're more endearing as well. Keep that in mind while you're shopping, and for heaven's sake think twice about rescuing an old piece instead of replacing it on a car you might own.

windshield and seats were available to round things out. To tailor the car to specific tracks— or just the specific needs of the driver—a standard or close-ratio gearbox could be combined with 4.09:1 or 3.77:1 rear-end gears.

The option game got very complicated over time, but it started out with some rather understandable packages:

Stage I consisted of a roll bar, antisway bars front and rear, and competition lap belts. Cost was approximately $280 over base price.

Stage II included Stage I options, plus magnesium wheels and flares, Goodyear racing tires, hood scoop and modified steering arms. The package ran about $1,225 over base.

Stage III combined the first two packages with chassis bracing, racing windshield, engine and rear-axle oil coolers, special shocks, steering arms, and antisway bars, racing brake pads and seats, jacking pads instead of bumpers, dual electric fuel pumps and larger fuel tank. Approximate cost was $3,505 over base price. (Option IV-R engine was mandatory.)

Commensurate engine packages could be bought as well; the Option II-R added four Webers, a larger oil pan, and polished valve covers for $254. Option III-R used dual four-barrels on a block that was Magnafluxed and balanced, a hot cam and distributor, strengthened pistons, rods, and crank, a set of ported and polished big-valve heads, a large oil sump, an aluminum intake manifold, and all attendant mountings and linkages for $1,907. Chuck on a set of four Webers in place of the dual quads and you had yourself an Option IV-R engine, worth $2,905.

Competition Cars

More than 85 percent of all small-block Cobras were never raced in a serious fashion, at least not until they became eligible for vintage racing much later in their lives. Of the cars that did race originally, it may be safe to say that no two are exactly alike today. Small numbers of them—two or three or even five —could have had the exact same specifications exiting the factory, but the strains of racing have by now made each one at least slightly different. New pieces were fitted to replace those that broke or proved otherwise unsatisfactory, each car received slight changes to suit its particular driver or owner, and they were simply modified and updated on an individual basis throughout their careers.

So what we have today are some broad categories of competition cars, but no 100 percent accurate description of how an individual model "should" be equipped. Fortunately, the histories of most leaf-spring racers are pretty well known by now by the SAAC.

Enthusiasts recognize three broad categories of small-block racing cars: team cars (those built and campaigned, or at least supported, by Shelby American); factory-prepared cars (those put together by Shelby American but campaigned by privateers); and independently prepared cars (those converted from street trim to racing trim by a private owner, team or shop).

Most of the cars in each category definitely belong there; some, however, are probably mislabeled. As more history is uncovered on each car, it's possible that a Cobra thought to be privately converted to racing trim might indeed have received that work at the factory or vice versa. (Recently found factory documentation shows some cars thought by their owners to be competition cars were not.)

The first Cobra racer, CSX2002, was driven by Billy Krause at Riverside, California, in October of 1962. It was as close to stock as any Cobra racer ever would be; a racing windshield, some hood louvers, a Spalding Flamethrower ignition kit, front brake scoops, a roll bar, and slightly wider wheels with Goodyear racing rubber pretty much summed up the changes. In that form, Krause walked all over the fuel-injected Corvettes running against him until a rear hub carrier broke. (All future Cobras used the billet-ground replacement that Phil Remington whipped up the next day as their prototype.)

The Cobra Goes Racing

The following paragraphs are not an attempt to present a complete listing of Cobra races and equipment. Our purpose is to show how the team cars evolved, and since street owners often copied the latest race car goodies, expect to find smatterings of all this equipment on many different cars.

Removing the windshield really adds a new line to the 289 Cobra, and a lot of street drivers did it very early on. On this legitimate B-Production racer, it's correct and desirable, but for the average street car it's merely dangerous. Replacement windshields and frames are expensive but necessary. *Nick Nicaise*

It's almost unbelievable that this was Ford's only demand in agreeing to become Carroll Shelby's engine supplier: a simple "Powered by Ford" plaque on the fenders of each car. On big-block cars there's a large "427" where the blue oval sits here—whether the car came with a real 427 or a 428. *Mike Lamm*

When rack-and-pinion steering came to the Cobra, a dished steering wheel also arrived. Like the earlier flat unit, it was rimmed in real wood, a nicety at the time but a potential source of grief today; the wheels can delaminate over time. *Nick Nicaise*

By the time Shelby American showed up at Nassau in the Bahamas in December 1962, a lot of things had changed from the basic specifications that outfitted Billy Krause's car. Now CSX2002 was joined by 2009, factory built but prepped and campaigned under Holman & Moody's banner, and CSX2011. Still derived from production models, these cars started looking more like racers. A roller cam and 12:1 pistons lived inside the engine, while straight-through side pipes handled the exhaust. Nine quarts of oil sat in the enlarged sump and a 37gal tank cut down on fuel stops. Hefty front and rear sway bars, an oil cooler, Koni shocks, front and rear brake scoops, a hood scoop and vents, alloy brake calipers, a roll bar, and stiffer springs were the main things separating these cars from their production brethren.

By January of 1963, CSX2026 and 2008 were taken somewhat further for competition at Riverside. To the basic package developed for Nassau, Shelby American added four Weber 48 IDM carburetors, twin master brake cylinders, a steering brace kit, external jacking pads, and a cold-air intake box. Naturally, all of these would be valuable options on a street car today.

Come Daytona in February, wide Halibrand magnesium wheels, headlight guards, larger rear fender flares and front fender spats, and modified steering arms appeared. The three-hour race was a washout for both Dan Gurney in CSX2002—the ignition on his hastily replaced engine went sour—and Skip Hudson in 2014, whose flywheel exploded and caused a serious crash. Dave MacDonald brought CSX2026 home fourth, behind two Ferrari GTOs and—heaven forbid—a Corvette. (CSX2014 would sit balled up in Shelby American's workshops until doing duty as the skeleton for sizing out the Daytona coupe's body panels.)

After stomping the competition at a small-potatoes SCCA event around Dodger Stadium in Los Angeles to get morale up, the team shoved off to Florida for the twelve-hour race at Sebring with some much-modified equipment. The cars were still hopped-up versions of street machines, but by now it was getting very difficult to tell. CSX2127 and 2128 were brand-new cars featuring 289ci engines and rack-and-pinion steering—both of which were soon to be fitted to Cobras across the board. Even wider flares graced the cars' rear fenders, and when they were running, the Cobras went like stink. Unfortunately, Sebring turned out to be a comedy of errors, and at the end of the race, only one Cobra—the Hill-Spencer-Miles CSX2127—was anywhere near the front of the pack at eleventh overall.

After Sebring, Shelby and AC started building competition cars from scratch; that is, cars were built with competition in mind from the outset rather than being converted from street specs after the fact.

The first cars to receive this treatment didn't get into the Shelby American stable at all, but were instead run by AC Cars (CS2131), Ed Hugas (CSX2142), and Willment Engineering (CS2130). Cobra CS2130 appeared first under John Willment's banner at Silverstone, and the two other cars followed at the 1963 running of Le Mans. They all featured side vents to duct hot air out from the engine bay, Dunlop magnesium wheels, a Shelby-built 289ci race engine with roller cam followers, and a sloping aluminum hardtop which aided aerodynamics and reduced driver fatigue. (Apparently the hardtop didn't justify the weight and trouble, as it wasn't adopted by Shelby American in later endurance events.) The car running under AC's banner finished the race in seventh place overall, behind six Ferraris.

The 24-hour effort got Ford thinking seriously about racing at Le Mans; after all, with relatively little time and money they had already finished second only to Ferrari. (Ford would learn over the next three years that pushing Ferrari down to the number-two spot was a considerably bigger task than imagined.) It also demonstrated the wisdom—if there had indeed been any doubt—of building certain cars from the outset as competition models. Shelby American saved themselves some trouble, and gained some valuable engineering freedom, by having AC start construction of certain cars with racing in mind.

Six more Cobras were built to roughly the same specs as those run at Le Mans, the group now known, predictably, as Le Mans Replicas. The first three (CSX2136-38) went directly into Shelby's racing stable; the rest were sold to favored privateers. Direct predecessors of the FIA (Federation Internationale de l'Automobile) and USRRC (United States Road Racing Circuit) cars that would be the ultimate leaf-spring roadsters, the Le Mans Replicas bridged the gap between the earlier modified street cars and the later all-out racers.

In addition to the usual go-fast Shelby goodies like a roller cam, competition brakes and ducting, stiff springs and thick antiroll bars, these cars also used the side vents that would show up on production cars after CSX2159, a steel accelerator pedal, and a cast-iron bellhousing. On all Cobras, the competition brake system is considerably more costly to repair than the relatively common street setup.

The year 1963 was the season for Shelby American to test the waters—which sounds a little odd considering they won the USRRC Manufacturer's and Driver's titles along with the SCCA A-Production crown. But 1964 was Shelby's season to turn up the heat, and to do that, a new generation of Cobras would be needed. (As new competition cars were made, one big difference separating them from their street-bound brothers was the variety of gauge layouts used. Often the "important" gauges for racing—tachometer, oil pressure, and temperature—were located ahead of the driver, and the speedometer was moved to the right in their place.)

Part of the teams' arsenal would be the Daytona coupes covered in a later chapter, but these played a relatively minor role in the points races of 1964. The next year, 1965,

CSX2473, considered by many the winningest Cobra of all time. An active B-Production racer from 1968 into the mid-1970s, its documented history makes it much more valuable than its hardware alone. *Nick Nicaise*

would be their year to shine. The mainstay of the teams' efforts would still be the roadsters, and two main series of cars evolved to take up the challenge: the FIA and USRRC Cobras.

Always built with a specific series in mind, the international FIA competitors wound up slightly different than the domestic USRRC cars. Five FIA (CSX2259, 2260, 2301, 2323 and 2345) and eleven USRRC competitors were constructed overall. Their most obvious features above and beyond the predictable Shelby racing hardware were exceptionally wide rear fenders over 7.5in (later 8.5in) wheels. This necessitated cutting back the rear edge of the doors somewhat and gave the cars a 427 Cobra-like profile. (The front fenders also grew as time went on, the last two receiving 427 style flares.)

The cars also featured unique dash layouts with speedometers swapping location with more important temperature and pressure gauges, a fiberglass racing seat for the driver, a degreed crank dampener, an electric differential fluid cooler, and a heat shield for the master cylinder assemblies. Two of the cars were stacked up—CSX2259 "beyond repair" at Sebring in 1964, and CSX2323 at Nurburgring in Germany, although like many Cobras they would surface again by virtue of their valued serial numbers. It is possible, however, that no parts or legitimate paperwork existed at the time the cars were "brought back."

In the meantime, six team cars were being built to USRRC specs, which varied from the FIA setup primarily in having a mechanical differential cooler. The cars were entered into 1964 races as they became available, and all six were at hand for the FIA season-ender at Bridgehampton, New York. Shelby American had just been "robbed" of the FIA GT title by Ferrari, and the Shelby team was out for blood. The ensuing Cobra festival made Bridgehampton look like a spec series.

Over the summer, five more customer cars were built to USRRC specs, although their primary venue would be SCCA Production racing and they were modified individually as rules and races warranted. The FIA and USRRC spec Cobras are second only to the Daytona coupes in history, performance and value.

The hippest Cobra wheel of all time could well be the pin-drive magnesium Halibrand knockoffs that were fitted to the USRRC and FIA racers, ultimately reaching 8.5in and 6.5in rear and front, respectively. Built exclusively for the Cobra—there's even a small Cobra lettering boss on the wheels—they necessitated major fender flares to stay covered. *Mike Lamm*

Very early 260 Cobra with small fender lips and no side vents. The smaller engine and worm-and-sector steering of these first cars made them slightly less sensational drivers than the later models, but their purity of line has kept values up. *Nick Nicaise*

This is the first Cobra ever built, with Carroll Shelby behind the wheel and his secretary (with gloves and a tiara) adding glamour to the photo shot by Dean Moon. The car, CSX2000, was assembled in Moon's shop and was run out to the local golf course for its first round of publicity shots. The body had been rubbed with steel wool in an effort to give it some shine, and it later was painted several times in different colors, one for each round of tests with magazine editors. *Dean Moon, courtesy of David Fetherston*

King Cobra

The AC Cobra was obsolete before it was even created. Don't get me wrong; it was absolutely the perfect tool for its intended job, more capable than even Carroll Shelby might have hoped. But in terms of winning out-and-out, run-what-ya-brung races, it just couldn't do it. Right before the Cobra came around, technology had relegated front-engined cars—in fact, *any* car that could be driven on both street and track—to also-ran status.

That was just fine as long as all you wanted was a GT (Grand Touring) championship, every SCCA win in sight, a streetable race car and to generally kick Ferrari's backside up and down the track at its own game. But to beat out the mid-engined, one- or two-off pure racers that appeared in the early 1960s, Shelby needed something more. What he got was the King Cobra.

Ultimately, this car was to be a weapon for 1964's USRRC title, which the factory Cobras

The new-think King Cobra led Shelby's organization into the mid-engined revolution. Some King Cobras are still missing out there, but identifying and verifying one at this late date could be almost impossible. Being racing cars, they're likely to have changed form so many times as to be almost unrecognizable. *Nick Nicaise*

Occasionally a Ford-engined middie shows up that *ought* to be a King Cobra but isn't. Dan Gurney's old Lotus 19, with a Shelby 289 (and Falcon/Cortina-style taillights!) doesn't qualify. *Nick Nicaise*

had swallowed up whole in 1963. But just about everybody realized that 1963 would be the last year a streetable race car could win the USRRC. There were too many middies out there, and a passable one was just too light and too fast for a superior Cobra to handle on a regular basis.

The King Cobra's heyday consisted of a popular but short racing series known as the West Coast Pro Series. The series appeared just as the SCCA was entering the field of professional racing, and it was among the first road-racing venues to attract big-name and big-buck racers to America. Shelby knew that an opportunity like that was too good to pass up.

Taking on the West Coast Pro Series would show what Shelby could do; it would give the team a chance to go up against the new breed of mid-engined cars, and it would be *fun*. The King Cobra probably came about as much

from Shelby-and-crew's sense of mischief as anything else.

What had worked before would work again. Shelby selected a top-notch European sports car that was doing just fine with a dinky European engine and stuffed in a Ford V-8. The recipient this time was the Cooper Monaco, a widened derivative of John Cooper's Formula One winner of a few years earlier.

Developed primarily for the latest Coventry-Climax four-banger, the Cooper wasn't quite as willing to take the Detroit iron as the AC had been. Some work and shoehorns convinced the Ford V-8 to fit. The rest of the car was pure Cooper thinking—triangulated tube frame, adjustable coil suspension at all four corners, four disc brakes, light alloy wheels. The engine was basically a racing Cobra unit, tuned with four Weber carbs and a cam profile that moved the power up the rev range to take advantage of the Cooper's light weight.

Strapped for time, two of the mid-engined Shelbys showed up for the opening race of the three-race West Coast Pro Series at Kent, Washington. Carroll and crew had hoped to pull a fast one on the competition, but when they arrived in Washington it became obvious that they weren't the only people with American-powered middies in mind. Shelby's cars overheated: Bob Holbert's dropped out right off the bat, and Dave MacDonald's failed after leading the race handily. The eventual winner was Lloyd Ruby in a Ford-powered Lotus 19, a mid-engined car built much along the Cooper's lines.

At Riverside, MacDonald won the race, and at Laguna Seca in Monterey, Holbert looked set to cream the field when a shunt closed off his radiator opening and led eventually to his retirement. MacDonald was struggling uncharacteristically at first, but he eventually got things sorted out and picked up the win when Holbert's King Cobra gave up the ghost. The King Cobras took the West Coast Pro Series in 1963.

Two more cars arrived from Cooper at the end of the year; one was dolled up for the Comstock Racing Team in Canada, and the other became a customer car for Craig Lang, heir to Olympia brewery dollars and an avid enthusiast. Lang's first car was balled up at Kent, Washington, by Bob Holbert and replaced by one of four more ordered from Cooper. Lang's new car received a unique Pete Brock-designed body and became known as the Lang Cooper, while the other three cars were finished in Shelby livery and

Shelby American added the huge hood air extractor when the King Cobras reappeared for 1964; engine cooling was always a problem with any big-engined middie, and these were no exception. The 289 Cobra engine and Colotti transaxle crammed into the back of the King Cobra both ran hot. King Cobra's winning days on the track were brief, and few people ever dreamed they would eventually become collectibles. *Nick Nicaise*

campaigned by the team. Parnelli Jones to-taled one of these at Laguna Seca in 1964.

The King Cobras were superb racing cars for their time, but as with any racer, their time was short. Faster and more sophisticated racers quickly appeared on the scene, and Shelby had his hands full with campaigning the small-block Cobras, struggling to get Ford's GT40 into line, and developing bigger fish like the 427 and the pending GT350. The mid-engine program was the least important iron in Shelby's fire, and the cars were sold off and raced by less wealthy and organized concerns.

Half of the eight King Cobras that passed through Shelby American can be accounted for: Bob Holbert and Parnelli Jones each removed one from the earth, one 1964 team car lives happily in Shelby livery, and the Brock-designed Lang Cooper was rescued from a junkyard and resurrected. That leaves four King Cobras unaccounted for.

How can four so important and valuable cars simply disappear? Easily. As pure racers, the King Cobras were built, cam-paigned, crashed, repaired, and eventually sold off as tools, not collector items. What mattered was that they ran as fast as they could, and if that meant stripping down the car and completely altering it from King Cobra specifications, so be it. Machines like these quickly became nothing more than used racing cars, and as they became less and less competitive, enthusiasts kept less and less of an eye on them.

Finding one of the lost King Cobras is a real Shelby lover's dream, but it could also become a nightmare. It's doubtful today that the missing cars would bear much resemblance to their former selves, and there were an awful lot of Cooper copies constructed in the 1960s, to say nothing of fourteen other Cooper Monacos built for customers other than Shelby American. All would be valuable to-day, but a true King Cobra would command the highest dollar.

All Cooper Monacos received a serial num-ber stamped onto a metal plate that was riveted to the dashboard. Although it's possi-ble that such a plate would remain today on these cars, modifications to this area would remove the ID plate and the fabricator proba-bly wouldn't bother reinstalling it. The serial numbers of the King Cobras are well known, too, and a forged plate would be an easy thing for an unscrupulous owner to cobble up. The chassis numbers, as assigned by Cooper, were as follows: CM/1/63, CM/3/63, CM/5/63, CM/6/63, CM/1/64, CM/4/64, CM/5/64 and CM/6/64.

The last twelve Cooper Monacos built were all specially fabricated to accept V-8 engines, and eight of these became Shelbys.

Daytona Coupe

Don't waste time daydreaming about discovering a Daytona forgotten in a barn. Six legitimate Daytonas were built, along with a couple of oddballs we'll get to later; all of them are present and accounted for. Assuming you've got a bank account the size of Pakistan's GNP, maybe you can wrest one from its owner. For the rest of us, the Daytona coupes are merely beautiful, fascinating racers to be admired from the pits when the Historics come to town.

The Daytonas came to pass when Shelby and friends decided to really go after the FIA Grand Touring championship, an international endurance racing series that took in courses like Le Mans, Sebring, Nurburgring, the Targa Florio, and Monza on the way to a world sports car title.

With the 1964 season looming, the Cobra had already proved it could mop up the American road-racing scene, but the (arguably) more prestigious European season was

Pete Brock's design for the Daytona Coupe was vindicated—and there were some doubters—by clinching the 1965 FIA GT title for Shelby American. CSX2300, shown, was involved in a transporter accident en route to its first race, the Tour de France in 1964; it didn't actually compete until Daytona, 1965. *Shelby American Automobile Club*

For a Pete Brock design, the Type 65 was frankly a tad on the homely side; its functional value won out over looks. Unfortunately, Shelby's later Lone Star mid-engined street project shared many of the Type 65's styling cues, and its appearance didn't inspire confidence in the rest of the project. (The Lone Star had mechanical problems that killed the project off as well.) *Nick Nicaise*

another matter. There the likes of Ferrari and Porsche were pouring tons of money every year into factory-backed teams with financing that rivaled that of Formula One racing. Tracks and races were generally longer and more varied across the pond as well, so racing in FIA GT meant learning a whole new set of rules.

If there was a single failing that would keep the Cobras from having an easy go of it, that failing was aerodynamics. FIA GT races often involved long straights and the sorts of top speeds that an SCCA driver only dreamed about. The Cobras had inherited early 1950s streamlining and, to put it simply, were about as slippery as the proverbial brick. That didn't matter much on the slower tracks usually found in America, but on the longer European courses it mattered a great deal. The Cobra muscled air out of its way with brute strength; a sleeker body to allow higher speeds and reduced fuel consumption from the same underpinnings might mean all the difference.

Late in 1963, the decision was made to build a slippery coupe body for the roadster chas-sis—a trick that would still qualify the coupes as production cars in the FIA's eyes. The rule was that as long as the innards remained stock, a car's body could be modified any way the builder liked. The Daytona's innards didn't turn out to be nearly as stock as the FIA had intended, but they were close enough; it was ruled to be a production Cobra, and therefore eligible to compete against Ferrari's all-conquering GTO for the Grand Touring championship.

(The GTO, to be fair, was already stretching rules beyond the breaking point. The FIA specifically stated that at least 100 vehicles of a type must be produced to make that car eligible for GT racing. Ferrari produced just enough cars to meet the needs of racing, then filled out bogus paperwork for the rest. Perhaps frustration at Ferrari's terminal hanky-panky led the usually persnickety FIA to allow the Cobra coupe.)

Using crude sketches and a slide projector to enlarge his drawings to full scale, Pete Brock designed an enclosed body for the Cobra on the wall of Shelby's shop. Brock, John Ohlsen and Ken Miles then oversaw the creation of a wooden forming buck on the chassis of CSX2014, the early racing roadster that self-destructed at Daytona with Skip Hudson aboard. The buck was sent to California Metal Shaping and aluminum panels were produced for the first (still unnamed) Daytona coupe.

Meanwhile back at the ranch, modifications were being performed on chassis CSX2287 to accept the new body. A triangulated tube structure was attached to stiffen things up and give the new cowl and roof something onto which they could be mounted. The radiator was tipped forward to allow for a lower hood-vented front end, and the driving position and steering wheel were sunk down to fit the driver into the low-slung cockpit.

There had been some controversy over whether "Brock's Folly" would do what he claimed—be faster than a stock 289 Cobra, stable at speed, or capable of running with the GTOs down the back straight. When the first test day at Riverside was over, however, no questions remained. The coupe was stable, solid, and notably faster than the standard Cobra—and, it seemed likely, the GTO as well.

The first race for CSX2287 was the Daytona Continental, and the car was trouncing the GTOs when a pit fire put it—and Shelby crewman John Ohlsen, who'd dashed under the car to look at an overheating differential—out of the running. Ohlsen and the car would both recover, but the coupe received a name that stuck: Daytona.

Several details were discovered during the race that would need attending to, most notably excessive heat in the cockpit, but the race was a typical Shelby first showing. With a little detail work, the Cobra coupe would obviously be a winner. Pete Brock was vindicated.

The second car, CSX2299, was a little different from the rest; somewhere along the way the cowl hoop was made 2in too tall, and the resulting bodywork was stretched out to fit it. If the car were being assembled at California Metal the error probably would have been caught and fixed. But the body was instead being made by Carrozeria Gran Sport in Modena, Italy, and the Italians received

Type 65 Super Coupe was scrapped before it got a chance to run the 1965 season, and the GT40 wound up taking Ford into sports car racing for the rest of the decade. Restoration more than fifteen years later finished off the car and brought it into racing trim, and it's the only one of its kind anywhere. *Nick Nicaise*

mismeasured prototypes all the time. They simply made the body panels fit the larger structure, and the result was 2in more of headroom. CSX2299 became Dan Gurney's car; it was the only one the lanky driver could fit into.

Gurney and Bob Bondurant took the taller Daytona to fourth overall, first in GT in the 1964 24 Hours of Le Mans, a finish that absolutely thrilled former Le Mans winner Carroll Shelby. And while Chassis 2299 and 2287 were giving Ferrari fits on their occasional 1964 appearances, three more coupes were being built by Gran Sport to bring the total to five.

Chassis number CSX2601 was originally intended to be a different animal: lengthened by 2in, it would carry a 427 into battle under a bulging hood. This potential conqueror was not to be, however. When the third coupe built, CSX2300, was smashed up in a transporter accident on the way to the Tour de France, 2601 was quickly converted back to 289 specifications. The Ferrari-Cobra war of 1964 was heating up and Shelby needed every available (and homologated) 289 Daytona to do battle.

Shelby's troops would eventually lose out to Ferrari that year, partly on the track and partly in the Italian ring of racing politics; but for 1965, the team would dive headfirst into the waters that had been tested tentatively. In 1964 the Daytona coupes collected points only occasionally, though they were entered at Daytona, Sebring, Spa, Le Mans, Rheims, Goodwood, and the Tour de France. And the roadsters were the real standard bearers of Shelby's effort. In 1965 it would be the other way around.

At the start of the season Shelby had five coupes in hand (CSX2287, 2299, 2601, the resurrected 2300 and 2602) and one more (CSX2286) in the pipeline. These were the weapons—along with Cobra roadsters on the

The long, relatively flat roofline and sharp Kamm cutoff was advanced but aerodynamically sound thinking. Adding the huge plexiglass rear window aided access and visibility while making the panel beaters' task a bit simpler. *Shelby American Automobile Club*

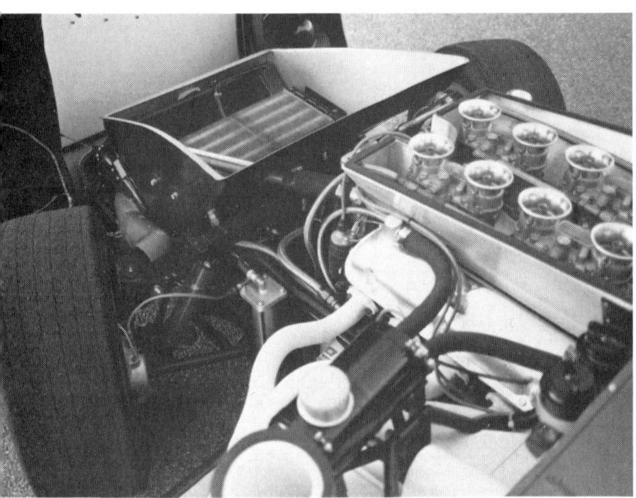

Full-race 289 with four Weber IDA carbs, oversized valves, forged pistons, and every available goodie from the Shelby parts bin put out about 385hp. The canted radiator necessitated some bracing that was distinctly un-Cobralike, but FIA's scrutineers let that one slide. Coupled with the tallest (2.72:1) rear axle available, the Daytona handily met Shelby's 180mph target. *Shelby American Automobile Club*

Deck-mounted spare still left a fair amount of room beneath the Coupe's hatch; like the Ferrari GTO before it, it doesn't take much imagination to see the Daytona as a viable tourer. CSX2300 temporarily sported a 302 and automatic transmission for just that purpose, and a few Daytonas were weekend drivers in the 1960s and 1970s. *Shelby American Automobile Club*

shorter tracks—with which Shelby American would handily win the 1965 GT title for the United States. The story of that fascinating season has been told many times (best, perhaps, by John Christy in *Carroll Shelby's Racing Cobra*). Although I won't retell the story here, suffice it to say, there was very little in the GT class that even came close.

After the 1965 season the Daytonas were sold off and their contemporary racing careers basically ended. At least one (CSX2300) competed ever-so-briefly in private hands, but for the most part they wound up in enthusiastic collectors' garages.

CSX2286 became one of the centerpieces of Larry Megibow's rather infamous demise; Megibow was considered a shady character who disappeared when the feds got close to an investment scam he was running shortly after purchasing the car in 1976. His "remains" were found in Canada, which threw the car's ownership into question until a living, breathing version of Megibow turned up as well a short time later. He died again— this time for good—the day before being sentenced, and his possessions, including CSX2286, were slated to be sold at an auction.

But that wasn't the end of it. The Daytona was stolen right before the auction by one of Megibow's less-savory business associates, and many feared that would be the last anyone saw of it. Fortunately, the car was found abandoned a little while later and was eventually sold into more reliable hands. One has to wonder, though, what the thief thought he could do with a hot Daytona— repaint it and file down the engine block?

Another coupe, CSX2287, wound up in the hands of John O'Hara, a low-profile man who originally had no intention whatsoever of selling the car. Eventually he did decide he could part with it, but buyers could never offer quite enough money to get it out of his hands. Each time a respectable offer came in, the price of the land O'Hara intended to buy with the money from the sale went up that much more.

O'Hara's wife got the car in a divorce settlement, but she continued to up the price just out of the reach of anyone who was interested in purchasing it; a modern fox-and-grapes fable that continues to this day. Wresting the car from the woman is something of a Holy Grail to some Cobra enthusiasts, but so far nobody's had much luck. Meanwhile, the car sits silently, corroding away.

The other four cars have led less juicy but nonetheless respectable lives, alternating between cherished private possessions, museum pieces, personal drivers, and vintage racers. Their histories are all well documented, and current owners—those who want to be bothered—can be found.

Now on to the few oddballs that deserve inclusion as Daytonas on the fringe. One was built by England's Willment Engineering with considerable help from John Ohlsen, who went to England to piece the car together on Carroll Shelby's OK. The Willment coupe at first appeared very similar to the other Daytonas, but over time more and more odd details sprouted on its body to differentiate it from the Shelby American animals.

Under the skin, however, the Willment coupe always featured a suspension and space-frame chassis unlike the other cars. It still runs proudly in English vintage events today. (This car should not be mistaken for CSX3055, a 427 chassis to which John Willment attached a 1950s era Ghia coupe body from a Fiat 8V. This car appears for sale every so often and confuses the heck out of people for months on end.)

The second oddball is the now-famous CSX3054 Type 65, Pete Brock's design for an all-enclosed, 427ci powered, coil-sprung car. The Type 65 began as a mega-Daytona, with engine, suspension, and aerodynamics that were supposed to take the Daytona concept into the next generation. Although a number of factors conspired to keep that from happening, two of them were most prominent. First, the British firm hired to construct the car, Radford Coachbuilders, was far from up to the task and took it on primarily as a way to

Pete Brock originally proposed a low-drag ring spoiler for the back of the Daytona, a racing standard today but unheard of at the time. Phil Remington decided instead to add a tried-and-true ducktail at Spa, which was not as advanced but worked just fine. *Shelby American Automobile Club*

Spartan interior was typical of race-car designs; excessive cockpit heat was the Daytona's primary trouble early on, a problem solved for the most part with side and cowl vents to remove engine heat before it went through the firewall. *Shelby American Automobile Club*

Relatively few modifications were required to Brock's excellent design after production. Small plastic vanes on the A-pillar broke up airflow around the cockpit and allowed the rear brake scoops behind the windows to function as intended, and the side vents were instrumental in keeping interior temperatures down. After being rediscovered in Japan and purchased by Carroll Shelby, CSX2300 was restored by Mike McClusky to 100 percent authentic condition. *Shelby American Automobile Club*

stay in Ford's stable—they were already constructing interiors for the GT40.

The other big hitch came when Ford money was withheld from the project; the GT40 Mark II program started coming together, and Ford felt that it was simply a more advanced design with more room for development. They were probably right; the Super Coupe would likely have had at most one season of glory before Ford and Shelby ironed out their more sophisticated car.

The Type 65 withered and died while Radford noodled around trying to get it built—or almost died, I should say. The semifinished car was eventually shipped back to Shelby where it languished in the shadow of other more promising projects. Little more than an oddity, it was finally sold into private hands.

But the car eventually wound up with Colorado enthusiast Craig Sutherland, who hired Mike Dopudja to finish it as Pete Brock had intended. Dopudja enlisted Brock's aid, and between the two of them the Type 65 was finally completed, more than fifteen years after it was supposed to debut. Gorgeously finished and sporting four Webers on its massive engine, CSX3054 at last turned a fast lap at the Riverside Historics in 1981. Needless to say, it went like stink. Maybe it wasn't so far behind the GT40 after all!

The third oddball is the wonderfully attractive AC coupe known as the A-98. Depending on whom you ask, the A-98 was developed strictly by AC with only inspiration coming from Shelby American, or with Shelby assistance through photos and phone calls. Regardless, the car was a lovely combination of Daytona, GTO and Mercedes 300SL styling influences that simply looked sensational and ran superbly.

Its first outing would be the 1964 Le Mans, but in prerace testing it went faster than 180mph—on public roads! Britain's traffic authorities were not amused, and after AC's little adventure it became considerably more difficult to get road registries for experimental racing cars in England. Regardless of Her Majesty's traffic cops, however, AC had shown that its car was at least as slippery as, if not more slippery than, Shelby's.

Where the Daytona was brutally attractive, the A-98 was elegant and sexy. Rumors started circulating about limited production, but it was not to be. A horrible sixth-hour crash at Le Mans involving the car killed three young spectators who had sneaked onto a restricted part of the course. After the deaths of the young fans, AC's decision not to pursue the car further is understandable.

The balled-up remains of the A-98 were eventually dragged out of AC's attic by English enthusiast Barrie Bird, who undertook a full restoration. Twelve years later it was finished. With its tragic past behind it, the A-98 has finally come back to the honored status it should have held all along. Bird deserves a lot of gratitude from Shelby fans for bringing the A-98 home again.

427 Cobra, street:	9
427 Cobra, S/C:	10
427 Cobra, competition:	10

427 Cobra

The Fastest Car in the World

To many people, the 427 is *the* Cobra to have. Featuring brutal good looks, a remarkably refined suspension, and enough torque and horsepower to light up a small city, it's the ultimate evolution of the big-engine, small-car idea that Carroll Shelby put to such good use in its predecessor.

But at the time it was offered, the 427 was far from the darling of the buying public.

Rod Leach's famous COB1 (actually COB6131). The car started out in Paramount's hands as the platform for a vehicle in the film *Those Daring Young Men in Their Jaunty Jalopies.* It was never used, though, and eventually Leach—who also owned the remains of Bill Cosby's twin-super- charged 427, CSX3303—decided to build it into *twin-turbo* 427 Cobra. COB1 doesn't have any historical significance at all, it's a complete hot rod; but at 700hp, it attracts attention regardless. *Nick Nicaise*

The single Holley carburetor with cold-air box frankly doesn't look all that impressive, but it's very correct and very, very effective. Excellent drivability, tremendous performance, and simple maintenance usually kept Shelby from getting too fancy when it came to intakes. *Nick Nicaise*

There were certainly people out there who wanted to have the fastest car on the road, but not as many as Shelby, Ford, and AC might have liked. Due to some unfortunate timing, there were also a lot fewer racing buyers than originally expected; when it came out, the 427 Cobra was not a big sales success. All 427 Cobras were built in Shelby American's Los Angeles International Airport (LAX) factory.

The car itself resulted more from an arms race of power and speed than any failing of the small-block Cobra. Carroll Shelby had two big concerns about the future as the 1964 season progressed. One was the rumored series production of the mid-engined Ferrari 275 LM; built in large enough numbers for GT racing, there was simply no way that the 289 Cobras could beat it. The other was the imminent stuffing of Chevrolet's big-block

The quick-fill aluminum cap on the 427's lovely derriere looks great, but if you're concerned about originality you'll have to make sure you know how it got there. This part is readily available on the aftermarket. *Nick Nicaise*

Vents flanking the grille are there to duct air into the cockpit on street 427s, and if the system isn't working right things can get pretty unpleasant inside. Suspect that they've been rerouted to the front brakes if the test drive becomes a real scorcher, though any 427 will toast your toes. *Nick Nicaise*

V-8 into the Corvette chassis. In bone-stock form, Chevy's big engine put out as much power as a full-race 289; jacked up for racing, the sky was the limit.

A bit less than 400hp was the absolute ceiling for a reliable 289, but there was another powerplant in the Ford collection that wasn't quite so constrained—the NAS-CAR (National Association for Stock Car Automobile Racing) 427 V-8. Ford had plenty of experience with this short-stroke 7.0 liter monster; it would kick out 500 horses all day long, requiring only great gulps of gas to keep it humming.

Ken Miles was the first to broach the subject of stuffing a larger, 150lb heavier big-block Ford engine into the Cobra chassis, back in 1963. Miles, famous for things like sticking Chevrolet V-8s into cycle-fendered MGs, got a happy nod from the boss, who wasn't about to stop Ken when he was on a roll.

And roll he darn near did. Miles took CSX2196, stripped off the body, buttressed up the frame and suspension, fabricated some motor mounts, and slotted in a 427 engine. After a Riverside testing jaunt next to the prototype Daytona, Miles added pin-drive magnesium wheels, plenty of cooling slots, a shabby-looking hood scoop and fender flares, and then carted the car to Sebring along with the regular Cobra racers.

The first big-block Cobra's outing was less than auspicious. Even with Miles herding the beast it proved to be a handful; in practice, he went off the track and nailed the only tree on the course, earning the name (behind his back, of course) of "Teddy Treebagger." After an all-nighter getting things back together, the car went out for the race but surprisingly blew its engine.

While running, Miles' hot rod slipped around the course like a Galaxie 500 with overinflated tires. When it did finally hook up, though, everyone could see there was definitely something to this big-block notion; the car shot forward like an Atlas rocket. CSX2196 was never going to be a winner, but the concept itself had definite merit.

Following the Sebring accident, Miles tried again with CSX2196, but this time he approached the problem differently. After stripping everything not *absolutely* mandatory off the car and fitting on a featherweight aluminum body—which hinged at front and rear to display the goodies—he slotted in an experimental aluminum Ford 390 with four huge Webers.

The 390 weighed about as much as a competition-spec 289, but made the power of a full-blown 427. Tipping the scales at about 1,600lb, the 390 competed against Chevrolet's Grand Sport Corvettes—themselves lightened and punched out to compete with the Cobras—and took them one better. At the 390's introduction at Nassau exactly one year after the Grand Sports had humiliated the Cobras there, Miles took off in the 390 and opened up a tremendous lead by the end of the first lap. As with his earlier big-block experiment, the lightweight 390 eventually expired before the end of the race; but it definitely gave the competition something to look forward to.

It came as a surprise to no one when Shelby gave Miles the nod to develop a production version of the Cobra featuring a 427ci engine. Miles' only guidelines were that the car must appear similar to the standard Cobra and mustn't cost Shelby or Ford a pile of dough to produce.

The first thing Miles did was widen the stock Cobra chassis and make it stronger, upping the mainframe rails from 3in to 4in in diameter and spacing them 5in farther apart

Ken Miles' lightweight 390, CSX2196, as raced at Nassau—one of the most collectible Cobras of all time. Miles stripped the car down to the bare essentials, added a unique flip-top front and rear body, and stuffed in an aluminum Ford big-block. The idea was to outdo the lightweight Chevrolet Grand Sport Corvettes which had humiliated the Cobras at the event a year earlier. The car didn't hold together, but it creamed the Grand Sports while it ran; a unique automobile with tremendous potential. *Nick Nicaise*

There's not much else that sits on its haunches like this, and it's no surprise the car has so many imitators. Each Cobra's body was formed by hand in aluminum, and it's doubtful that any of them were ever as straight and nice as this from the factory. With prices being what they are today, however, the average quality of Cobras is a lot higher twenty-five years down the road than it was on the showroom floor. Today a buyer of a show car must be willing to spend enough for a car that's perfect, not just original. *Nick Nicaise*

to clear the wider engine. Finally given a chance to dump the aging transverse leaf suspension, Miles and Company did just that, replacing it with independent and adjustable coil-sprung units at all four corners.

As the design progressed, the new Cobra evolved very differently from the old. Until now, Shelby had been having great success building cars more or less as he went along: starting with a good idea, testing it, breaking things, and patching up the holes until he got the machine he wanted.

But this time Ford's computers were brought in to solve many of the technical details before they were ever committed to metal. Ford's Klaus Arning oversaw a gaggle of enthusiastic Ford Motor Co. employees who ran simulations and equations for the new car on their own time. The result was a tremendously powerful street and racing car that required very little debugging once the first few were built. In theory, the 427 Cobra simply shouldn't have worked very well; too much weight up front, not enough room for the engine, too little traction, too willowy a frame, and so on. In practice, it worked like a dream.

Very little of the old car remained. The 427 was 7.0in wider than the 289, 4.5in longer and of course heavier—though only by a claimed 250lb. (That figure may be suspect. The car's brakes, wheel carriers, halfshafts, just darn near *everything* became bigger and beefier than before.) No matter what the actual difference, it was more than compensated for by the bigger car's 138 spare cubic inches and 100-150 additional horsepower.

Shelby's original plan was to complete 100 cars in time to certify the 427 Cobra for the FIA's 1965 season. By the time the FIA inspector made it out to Shelby American, though, only fifty-one cars could be shown and homologation was withheld. That being the case, Shelby notified AC Cars to start immediately on production of street-spec 427s.

About a dozen 427 race cars had been completed by Shelby and shipped out to privateers by mid-summer 1965. The first car off the factory line (CSX2701, later retitled CSX3001 when the decision was made to give all coil-sprung cars a CSX3– designation) went straight to Ford for evaluation and photos. CSX2702, later retitled 3002, was finished off by Shelby in Viking blue and white and prepared for competition. It would be Shelby American's only 427 factory racer. Its original role was to be the development mule for the expected 100 competition cars.

The two vehicles already mentioned were built before legitimate 427 body bucks could be constructed, so 2in wide strips of metal were sectioned into the fenders of 289 FIA-style bodies to cover the wider chassis. The story of the earliest cars aside, after the FIA's homologation papers were withheld, Shelby American had a problem. The remainder of the fifty-two competition cars already made, intended for racing customers who now would not materialize, were suddenly dead

wood. The situation did not improve as summer turned to fall, and by November there were still more than thirty full-race cars ready to be finished and sold; bearing a price tag of well over $9,000 a crack, they didn't look to be going anywhere soon.

As mentioned, these cars were not quite finished—for that they had to wait until a customer order came in, when the final touches like paint and wheels were applied. But if these cars were not being sold to racers, reasoned Shelby's eastern sales representative Charles Biedler, why not sell them for use on the street? The 427 S/C (for Semi Competition or Street/Competition, depending on who's answering the question) was born, and it was a good idea. Billed as the fastest production vehicle of all time, the 427 S/C program soon cleared out Shelby's lots.

Meanwhile, the street-car program did not go without its hitches either. Three street prototypes, CSX3101, 3118, and 3120 (all street cars received a CSX31– or higher serial number) were flogged by Shelby American to

Very wide rear flares and rectangular taillights mark this as a relatively early example of the 427 line. Rectangular taillights were notoriously hard for other drivers to see, a fact which early 427 drivers should bear in mind while driving on the street. *Nick Nicaise*

work out the inevitable hitches. Predictably the first problem was cooling, as the huge engine put out tremendous amounts of heat and the only place it could go was into the cockpit.

The engine temperature itself was brought into line primarily by an electric fan ahead of the radiator. Inside the cockpit, revised insulation and ducting solved the problem for the most part. The openings on either side of the grille vented cool air into the cockpit on street cars, but on racers that air went to the front brakes. Either way, the intrusion of heat into the driver's compartment was never entirely tackled. Toasty driver's toes would be the norm for every 427 Cobra made.

The other steps of the debugging process are more minor. Throttle linkages had to be built up, the crowded driver's side exhaust manifold needed reworking, and other small fixes needed attention. Altogether, though, the modifications required were strikingly small—Shelby's people and Ford's computers had done an excellent job in getting things right the first time.

The real hitch in 427 production turned out to be something that even Ford's electronic brain couldn't predict: wheels. The cars were supposed to feature pin-drive magnesium Halibrands like the ones used on Ford's GT40s. Halibrand couldn't build the wheels fast enough, though, so street-car sales were held up for lack of equipment just as competition car sales were held up by lack of an FIA certification.

Pete (of-all-trades) Brock quickly drew up the ten-spoke aluminum Sunburst wheels that later became a Shelby American specialty; but these *too* were briefly held up by production problems at Halibrand, which was again the supplier. Finally the wheels came on line and the cars could start moving out the door, but not until some valuable sales had probably been lost for good.

Road testers who had raved about the 289 Cobras must have at first approached the 427 variety with some trepidation. After all, the earlier car was brutish enough with considerably less weight and horsepower, so the 7.0liter was sure to be a true handful. In many ways it was: the big-block car did not suffer fools lightly, and it always called for

Twin Holleys under their own air cleaners weren't as attractive as those sporting a single oblong Cobra case, but their effectiveness was unchanged. Braided lines and plated tank are not original. *Nick Nicaise*

judicious use of the throttle. But at least to the decent drivers who made up most of the press corps, the bigger car redeemed itself through absolutely shattering performance, its refined suspension, surprisingly light controls, and the wider, more comfortable cockpit.

---

427 Cobra Chassis and Body Integrity

Since the 427 shared the same basic body and chassis as the 260 and 289 covered earlier, those comments apply to 427 Cobras as well, with the following exceptions:

- There is no ID tag correlation between 427 chassis and engine blocks.
- Reproduction 427 steering wheel centers are red, white, and blue, but the situation is the same for these as for the black and silver 289 buttons— repros are out there, but they're not great.
- All 427 Cobras use Smiths gauges of a different type than the early 260 Cobra Smiths units. The ammeters, however, are inexplicably almost always made by Lucas—that's normal.

Lower scoop for oil cooler was deleted after CSX3300. The scoop was simply too easy to smash up on curbs and driveways, and street vehicles didn't have an oil cooler to feed anyway. *Nick Nicaise*

It was not a car for timid or simply bad drivers, however, and that's something that today's buyer must realize. Because of its performance potential, things can and do happen fast in a 427 Cobra. The tail of the car will break loose in a notoriously easy fashion, and all that engine up front can cause some interesting responses in fast cornering. The car is *not* inherently dangerous—in fact, far from it. The trouble is simply that its performance can goad the inexperienced driver into stupid mistakes. Whether or not the 427 is an easier car to drive than the small-block Cobra is a matter of taste; that it is considerably faster is not open to discussion.

Magazine road testers did find things to complain about, the car's odd shifter location prime among them. And those who didn't treat the 427 with the respect it deserved came back with harrowing tales of mid-

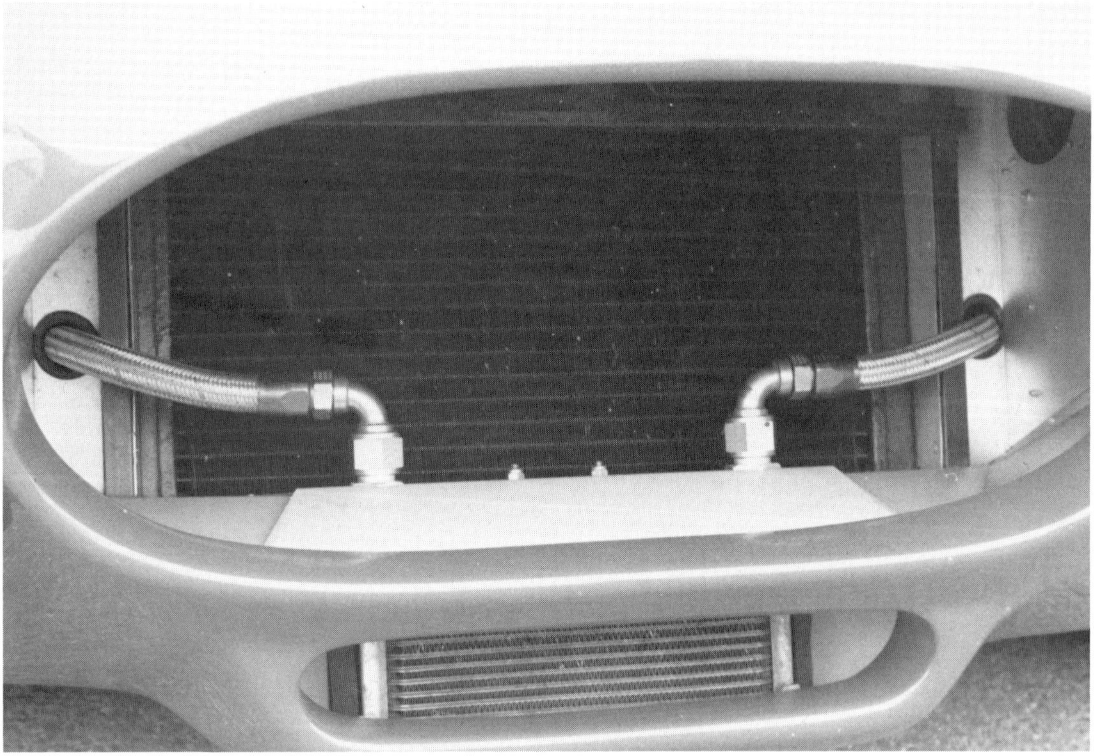

Clean installation of the oil cooler on 427 S/C and competition models justified the second scoop featured on all 427s prior to CSX3301. A lot of coolers in this location have been tremendously banged up by stones over the years and some have even ruptured. This one looks very nice, though. *Mike Lamm*

corner—and even mid-straight!—spins, and the general feeling that it was a monster waiting to attack. Those who handled the car correctly, however, had nothing but praise. There was nothing, anywhere, that was likely to outrun the 427 Cobra, and the fact that it was also predictable to a good driver was just gravy.

427 S/C, Competition and Street Equipment

The street car initially sported a true NAS-CAR-derived 427ci top-oiler V-8 with one four-barrel carburetor mounted on a low-riser intake manifold, a cast-iron block and heads, Ford exhaust manifolds, 10.4:1 compression, and solid lifters. Horsepower was factory rated at 425bhp, which was generally regarded as a conservative figure. The 427 S/C appeared, when not sporting a full-competition engine, with a medium-riser intake manifold sporting two fours, an oil cooler, and enough other engine goodies to make a noticeable improvement in performance. The full-competition-spec engine—with medium- or high-riser intake manifold, a single four-barrel in an aluminum air box mated to the hood scoop, an extremely valuable set of heavily worked-over aluminum heads (which often failed and were replaced with easier-to-get iron heads), 12.4:1 compression, lightweight valvetrain parts, tubular straight-through exhaust system, oil cooler, and other goodies—measured in at a definitely conservative 485hp.

It's important to remember that while hardware generally trickled down from these models—that is, S/C pieces were commonly ordered on street cars—it rarely went the other way. Thus a street-specification part on a purported S/C or full-competition platform should be viewed with suspicion.

The 427 Cobra S/C was potentially every bit as competitive as the full-spec racer. Since the cars were finished one at a time for specific buyers, many differed only in the most trivial ways from the all-out racing cars; naturally, quite a few wound up on the track. In general, the S/C models differed from the racers by having just a touch of muffling stuck in their side pipes, rubber suspension bushings instead of bronze, and GT40- rather than FIA-

Unique S/C dash layout is correct, reflecting race driver's relative indifference to mph figures. Though almost all of the S/C equipment could be added by request from Shelby or after the fact, street dashboards were never modified to copy this layout at the factory. *Nick Nicaise*

style magnesium Halibrands. (The S/C wheels were in fact an inch wider all around than those on the GT40.) The S/C models also had cooling fans, which were absent on the competition cars.

Other than that, both types shared much which separated them from the street cars. Aside from the intake, exhaust, and internal engine differences mentioned earlier, the race- and S/C-spec cars made front and rear antiroll bars standard, had twin aircraft batteries behind the passenger's seat, slightly larger rear discs, a 3.77:1 (versus 3.54:1) Salisbury rear end, electric booster fuel pumps, different instrumentation and dashboard layout (the important oil pressure and water temperature gauges were in front of the driver and the speedometer was moved to the center panel—a fuel pressure gauge also appeared), jacking pads in lieu of tube bumpers, 42gal (versus 18gal) fuel tanks, 13qt Aviad oil sumps and aluminum (rather than fiberglass) trunk trays.

Cobra brakes get a tremendous workout, so it's a good idea to give the calipers and rotors a really thorough checkout before buying—and check them frequently after the car's in your garage. Standard Cobra braking systems are pretty easy to repair and find parts for, the more exotic racing layouts much less so. *Nick Nicaise*

Big, brutish 427 hood scoop was in fact a factory piece. A wide variety of scoops was needed to cover the various intake systems which could be specially ordered from Shelby American, so there's no single correct unit. *Nick Nicaise*

With this much in common with all-out racers, expect to find many legitimate Cobra S/Cs showing evidence of competition.

Many owners have modified street-bound Cobras to S/C specifications, of course, and from the driver's standpoint maybe there's nothing wrong with that. From the investor's standpoint, however, a fake S/C isn't a good idea unless it's priced well below the real McCoy. On balance, a production 427 that's been turned into an S/C is worth less, even after selling off the goodies, than one that's been left alone.

Even in its "tamest" production form, the 427 had considerably more power than could be used in everyday driving. Midway through the production run it was replaced in the street cars with Ford's less exotic, 390hp 428ci Police Interceptor engine, still fitted with solid lifters and surprisingly efficient Ford exhaust manifolds. Even those 390 horses were more than about 95 percent of drivers could actually use, and the engine resulted in a performance drop that was marginal at best off the racetrack. Shelby received very few complaints on the car's performance no matter what type of engine was used.

The decision to use the 428 was, of course, a financial one. A 427 side-oiler cost over $700 from Ford, while the 428 was more than $400 cheaper. At a time when Ford was questioning the need to lose money on every 427 Cobra sold, Shelby American used the 428 as a token that they were at least trying to keep costs down. But while most street drivers couldn't care less—and could order the 427 anyway if they really wanted it—the 428 remained something of a bone in Carroll Shelby's throat.

The 427 was reinstated before the end of street-car production, but the exact serial numbers receiving either engine were not collated. The best rough estimate is that *most* CSX32– cars received the 428, the engine *generally* ran two four-barrel carbs versus the 427's single unit, and the owners' eyeballs got flattened either way.

Today, however, it's not so simple; a legitimate and original 427 is a selling point. The best way to tell which engine a car has is by the 427's main-bearing cross bolts—this en-

Computer-designed suspension does allow a degree of body roll, and the 427 could be very hard to recover if it sprung back and overcorrected a slide.

Quadruple Webers on a 427 Ford are probably the ultimate expression of overkill, but they're out there nonetheless. With the twin Holley setup already capable of flowing more fuel than the 427 Cobra could ever use—and it could use a lot—eight throats of Weber carburetion can only be seen as an aesthetic, rather than functional, addition.

Side by side, the differences between the 289 and much wider 427 really become apparent. There's a lot of extra meat in the 427's fenderline, but until you look at them together it can be a little tough to tell. All that extra size, of course, meant extra weight, but there was so much more engine in the 427 that the difference was handled and then some. *Nick Nicaise*

gine has three large bolts equally spaced along each side right above the oil pan, while the 428 has none. (After Shelby convinced Ford that selling cars called 427s with 428 engines was not the greatest idea in the world, a real side-oiler 427 reappeared for the rest of the run—meaning *most* CSX33– cars had it.)

A few other running changes help to break up the 427 Cobras into more manageable groups. Of 348 total coil-spring cars, 260 (numbers CSX31– and higher) cars were built for street use. Thirty-two were COB6– and COX6– cars not sent to America powered by 289 V-8s. Thirty-one were Cobra S/C models, while twenty-one wound up in competition form, all receiving CSX30– serial numbers and competition-style rear fender flares. Four were built as chassis only, and of these CSX3054 became the Super Coupe as discussed earlier. 3055 received an old Ghia body at the hands of John Willment, 3063 received a new one-off body from Ghia, and 3027 was eventually finished off privately as an S/C long after production ceased.

All cars prior to CSX3201 had rectangular taillights; after that, two round lights came on line. At CSX3301 the oil cooler scoop disappeared from beneath the grille, and cars CSX3125–3158 had relatively restrained rear fender flares—the rest of them had the heavier wide flares normally seen on the car. Four cars received automatic (Lincoln spec) transmissions, two of them special dual-Paxton-supercharged monsters for Carroll Shelby (CSX3015) and Bill Cosby (3303); the other two, both normally aspirated, were specially ordered and built. Shelby executive (and fine driver) Al Dowd had something of a misadventure—a mid-highway spinout on downshifting—in a prototype 427 automatic, so by and large Shelby American wasn't too hot on the idea.

427 Cobra in Competition

The 427 Cobra wasn't FIA GT legal in 1965, and by 1966 Ford's GT40 program was up and running well. The result was that just one 427 Cobra, CSX3002, was ever a "factory" competition car.

Ironically, the big-block Corvette threat never emerged and Ferrari couldn't homologate the 275 LM; the upshot was that 289

Beautiful cast aluminum Cobra 427 rocker cover is a valuable addition in place of the more common stamped and chromed variety. This is a somewhat rare piece you're not likely to come across often. *Nick Nicaise*

Cobras had no trouble at all securing the 1965 FIA GT World Championship. The second irony is that despite its potentially superior performance, 427 Cobras never achieved anything like the racing successes that Shelby attained with the small-block cars. This is directly attributable to a lack of Shelby American development and support, the result of the cars' not qualifying in any class in which Shelby was actively racing. Debugging and modification was left to privateers with what little help Shelby could offer, given their lack of experience with the cars.

Nevertheless, the 427 Cobra did go on to a fine career in domestic SCCA A-Production racing—which is probably what it was best suited for all along. (The SCCA, unlike the FIA, granted the car production status after seeing a single prototype. They knew that if

Carroll Shelby said he'd series-produce the car, it was as good as done.)

In the SCCA, the 427 Cobra would compete with other street-based automobiles, not mid-engined, pure-race specials. It arrived at a time when race cars and street cars were finally and irrevocably going their separate ways, and in truth the SCCA would be one of the last holdouts of the dual-purpose sports car.

Competing on basically equal footing with other privateers in the class, the 427s ruled the roost in production racing until almost the end of the decade. Corvettes took over from 1969 to 1972, but Sam Feinstein finally took the A-Production championship back with CSX3009, a car that had already been racing for more than eight years.

Cast magnesium GT40-style Halibrands were applied to the 427 when available (shown), but often the Sunburst (also made by Halibrand, but to Pete Brock's design) wheel had to be fitted instead. Excellent replicas of both wheels are now available, mostly for kit cars. *Nick Nicaise*

Chapter 5

1965-1966 GT350

1965 GT350:	8.5
1965–'66 GT350R:	9
1966 GT350:	8
1966 GT350H:	8
1966 GT350 convertible:	9

1965 Shelby GT350

The Ford Mustang was the sales success of the decade—of a lot of decades, in fact—when it was introduced in the summer of 1964. Though basically just a rebodied and warmed-over Falcon, the new 2 + 2 was pouring off the production line and straight out the showroom door. Lido A. "Lee" Iacocca's smiling face made the cover of *Time* magazine—and it wouldn't be the last time—alongside his sporty progeny; there were other men who probably deserved the title Father of the Mustang more, but none who fit the part as well as Iacocca.

The Mustang was a hot car, Iacocca was a hero, and Ford wanted more: more sales, more PR, and more niches into which to slot the new Mustang. To achieve all these they realized they needed more performance, or perhaps more accurately, more of a *performance image* for the car. Building a few really hot Mustangs would rub glory off on the rest, and drive the guys over at Chrysler and GM nuts to boot.

Oblong vents in the front valance were introduced on the later R-model Shelbys. Most aftermarket valances use the smaller round openings, which didn't flow as much air to the brakes. *Nick Nicaise*

Who better could Ford have turned to for that performance boost than Carroll Shelby? After all, Shelby was already winning lots of races and PR with what was generally thought of as a Ford product, and the Cobra's laurels far outweighed Dearborn's investment.

In fact there was one other place Ford could have gone, and originally they did: to the Ford Motor Co. itself. Ford's large and talented engineering department knew a thing or two about making cars go fast, and the original plan was to create a super Mustang in-house. Dearborn's engineers cobbled up an independent rear suspension for the Mustang while the front office started wooing the SCCA to let the car into a class it could dominate. Unfortunately, the SCCA wasn't biting.

That's when Ford turned to Carroll Shelby, and realized that the plan made a lot of sense.

Ford already knew that Shelby could build very fast street cars; they knew he could win races; and they knew that the cachet of Shelby's name would only help to get that racy image that Ford was looking for. Ford must have also known, in truth, that if something really horrible came of the hot Mustang it would be Shelby, not the company, who'd take most of the heat. But such a scenario was unlikely in Shelby's capable hands. His small nucleus of talent could whip up a vehicle for less money and in less time than Ford's behemoth organization, and it was a pretty sure bet to *work*.

In August of 1964, Shelby's Cobra Mustang project got rolling. Because he knew that racing would be the key to setting up the image Ford wanted—and because he just liked to go racing—one of Carroll's first stops was a friendly little visit to John Bishop's office at the SCCA. Bishop laid out what would be

Five-spoke magnesium wheels may well have been added by the dealer before this Shelby was delivered, but the Shelby ten-spokes on the GT350 right behind it make that a more valuable car.

Always try for the original Shelby equipment when you can, or you may have to hunt the pieces up later. *Nick Nicaise*

required to turn a Mustang into a B-Production racing car. First, two of the seats would have to go. Second, 100 examples would have to be built before the first of January 1965. And third, competition versions of the car could have modified engines or suspensions, but not both—which meant Shelby's homologated "street" version would have to feature one or the other on all 100 cars.

Getting rid of the rear seat would be no problem, Shelby knew, and making 100 cars by the first of the year could be done. (For the Ford bureaucracy it might have been impossible, but for Shelby, no trouble.) That simply left the decision to sell the customer versions with a racing engine or a racing suspension—and then to develop the whole package in no time flat.

The engine-suspension choice was easy. It would be a lot safer to guarantee a racing suspension than a racing engine, so the die was cast. With the suspension homologated as stock, Shelby could fiddle with the engine for his racing cars.

He acquired two notchback Mustangs and handed them to Ken Miles on a platter. Miles was told to go away, play with the cars, and bring them back as racers. Furthermore, he

SAAC head Rick Kopec's own R-model is frequently seen as Rick cleans out the engine across the country. There's not much chance of prying this one away, but legitimate R-models like it do sometimes come up for sale. They aren't ever cheap. *Nick Nicaise*

was told, don't do anything too expensive in the process—use as many Ford production pieces as possible, and spend money only where it counts.

Bob Bondurant and Miles, with some help from Klaus Arning's computerized suspen-

The big gap in the plexiglass rear window of the R-model helped smooth airflow over and through the car, an early example of clever aerodynamics. Almost no one has bothered to fake this on street cars, so the open backlight can be one of the fastest identifiers of a true R-Model Shelby. R-Models and any other high-strung Shelbys put enormous strain on the engine's lower end, so be wary of ominous rod knocks and filings in the oil. *Nick Nicaise*

sion boys, spent long workdays at Willow Springs in Rosamond, California, with the notchbacks, cutting and pasting in suspension components until the two Mustangs began acting less like Sunday drivers and more like Sunday racers. When they finally got the setup dialed in the way they wanted it, they went back to Shelby American and told the crew what had to be done.

Shelby assimilated the information and then made his order from Ford's San Jose assembly plant. He wanted about 100—it would eventually be 115—Mustang fastbacks built to a certain specification. The cars would all have Hi-Po 271hp 289 engines, four-speed aluminum-case Borg-Warner T-10 gearboxes, white exteriors with black interiors, 11in vented Kelsey-Hayes front discs with competition pads, and 9in rear ends with Detroit Locker limited-slip differentials. Furthermore, certain parts were to be deleted during assembly: hoods and latches, grilles, emblems, exhaust systems, rear seats, and radios.

While San Jose was completing the two-day build, two other bits from the Ford parts bin were added on the line: the so-called export brace, which ran from the firewall to the shock towers and appeared on all Mustangs intended for foreign sale, and extra-wide Fairlane station wagon rear drum brakes.

After playing with the two previously acquired notchbacks, Pete Brock had already taken care of the external treatment of the new cars. After struggling with emblems for a Cobra Mustang, the decision had been made —or pulled out of thin air—to call the car GT350. Brock easily fit the nomenclature into the blue rocker stripes already planned. Matching blue Le Mans stripes over the top of the car were also a natural. The Le Mans stripes were technically an option, alternately factory- and dealer-installed, but only one-

Getting this B-Production Shelby back to mid-sixties specifications would be an expensive proposition. As a modern race car it's one thing, but to be an original Shelby the flares, spoiler, windshield, etc. would all have to go. *Nick Nicaise*

Dash-mounted tach introduced in 1966 helped to bring cost of the GT350 down; some of them have led the surrounding dash panel to crack in the years since, however. *Nick Nicaise*

Paxton supercharger, driven by a belt off the engine, fed pressurized air into a sealed housing around the carburetor. Buyers could specify this unit on the order sheet, but the cars generally arrived with all the hardware in the trunk unless the dealer himself could be cadged into installing it. *Nick Nicaise*

third of 1965 cars got them at the factory in any case. In place of the rather silly looking horse and corral in the standard Mustang grille, the GT350 had a single Mustang fender badge located on the driver's side of a plain grille opening. A fiberglass hood with an integral scoop and hood pins further distinguished the car from stock.

Shelby had a fair bit of trouble with the fiberglass—and that would happen again later—so at about the halfway point of 1965 production a steel bracing system was adopted to alleviate cracking.

In the meantime, the hood springs were removed and a prop rod appeared in their place, to take some of the tension off the hood's rear quarters. So when inspecting any Shelby, give the hood a good hard look before buying the car. Look for large cracks around the edges, scoop, and especially the hinges and pins; small stress cracks are pretty easy to fix, but delaminated cracks are a big problem. (On the rarer 1966 all-steel hoods, look for waves, metal cracks around the scoop, and bad edges.)

The stock wheels were unglamorous but honest stamped-steel 15x5.5in Kelsey-Hayes units, unremarkable except for a small K-H stamped into their backsides. Optional was a Cragar five-spoke 15x6.0in aluminum and chrome wheel with CS-logo center cap. Spe-

cially constructed Goodyear (who else?) Blue Dot tires, 7.75x15, were standard equipment.

The first three GT350 prototypes were basically made by hand with a lot of unique machined parts. SFM5S003, the first of the lot, was the prototype for the street cars while SFM5R002 and SFM5R001 were prototypes for the race-only R-model discussed later in this chapter.

I mention these cars mostly as a sneaky way to get into the GT350's numerology, which is something of a science of its own. As cars were unloaded from the San Jose transporters and moved into the Venice factory, no attempt was made to correlate or construct them in order of their Ford VIN numbers. The Ford numbers were stamped twice on the driver's side inner fender (one number was visible and the other was hidden until the fender came off), once on the engine block, and once (again hidden until removing the sheet metal) on the passenger's side inner fender. The Ford VIN of a real 1965 GT350 should begin 5R09K: 5 for 1965, R for the San Jose assembly plant, 09 being the code for a two-door fastback, and K designating original installation of the 289 Hi-Po V-8 engine.

After completion, Shelby pop-riveted a special identification plate over the visible Ford plate on the driver's side fender and stamped the same number into the passenger's side inner fender panel. The number begins SFM5S (*Shelby Ford Mustang, 1965, Street*) or SFM5R (*Shelby Ford Mustang, 1965, Race*) followed by a three-digit job number *approximately* reflecting that car's place in the production run.

Still with me? OK, now hold on to your hats: Cars previous to SFMS032 did *not* use an S or R designation, with the following exceptions: the first three prototypes, SFM5S003, SFM5R002, and SFM5R001, didn't actually receive their VIN stamps until they were sold to the public near the end of 1965 production. Therefore, these very valuable cars do have the later S and R designations—which may confuse anyone wealthy enough to consider buying one of them.

But wait! Those numbers are *still* a bit erroneous. SFM5R002 and SFM5R001 are actually numbered in the reverse order of completion. (A mechanic made the mistake when attaching the plates, and nobody figured it mattered much on a couple of old race cars.) Incidentally, the SAAC keeps a record, under

wraps, of Ford VINs as they correlate to Shelby VINs, and they'll tell you whether the two sets on a given car are a match or not. But the SAAC does not "give out" Ford VINs. It will only confirm or deny VIN info people submit. It's a good idea to contact them with both VINs before buying any GT350, but bear in mind that a dedicated forger can lay his hands on enough information to fool even some experts, so read up on fakes and air cars at the back of the book.

Now let's plow our way back out of the murky depths of VIN numbers and get into the more enjoyable business of hardware. Of the changes Miles and his cohorts developed, the two biggest had to do quite naturally with major suspension modifications. At the back, overriding traction bars were installed to combat the Mustang's notorious rear-axle hop. To install the traction bars, the entire rear end of the car had to be removed so the appropriate mounting brackets could be welded up underneath. The forward mounting points of these bars actually went *inside* the passenger compartment, so after the work was done a fiberglass box and rubber gaiter were riveted and sealed around them to keep out fumes and water. Check closely for corro-

Standard competition-width lap belts are tough to come by nowadays. *Nick Nicaise*

Most 1966 Shelbys merely added a unique GT350 center cap to the standard Mustang rally steering wheel, though a real wood wheel sometimes does appear. Good but not perfect reproductions of the center cap are available. *Nick Nicaise*

sion and dampness in this area to avoid costly floor replacement later.

Adjustable Koni shocks were also added at the rear, and wire cables were attached to the axle by eyebolts to prevent it from traveling too far when unloaded and pulling the rear shocks from their mountings (because they had slightly insufficient travel).

Up front even more drastic measures were called for. The coil springs were removed at Shelby American to allow access to the upper A-arms, which were then lowered 1in by drilling new pickup points and remounting the assembly. Another set of Koni adjustable shocks went on at the front, along with a 1in antiroll bar, new idler and Pitman arms, and a Monte Carlo bar—a steel tube that tied the front shock towers together for strength. The longer Pitman and idler arms cut the steering ratio down from 22:1 to a much more respectable 19:1; this made fast street driving much more pleasant in the GT350 than the regular Mustang.

The area where the rear seats would be on a normal Mustang was covered by a fiberglass panel to which the spare tire fixed, and an 8000rpm tachometer (with a CS logo) and oil pressure gauge were mounted in a dedicated plastic housing which fit the middle of the dashboard's top edge. (Caution: Both the dash and housing can warp and crack after sitting in the sun for more than twenty-five years.) Three-inch competition-style lap belts held occupants in place, and the belts' mounting bolts also ran through the floorboards to secure a driveshaft retaining loop in case of U-joint failure.

The first 100 or so GT350s got real 16in wooden steering wheels like the ones used on the Cobras, the spokes of which are varied due to manufacturer changes. It was quickly noticed, though, that the 16in wheel banged into many drivers' thighs, so once the 100-odd supply ran out they were replaced with 15in wheels to allow for more room; here too a number of different types were used seemingly at random. The horn button was moved to a spring-loaded toggle switch on the dash—much to the surprise of a few panicked owners and test drivers.

Standard Ford trunk mat and filler neck parts are all readily available in the aftermarket. As long as the trunk itself is sound, this area shouldn't cause a restorer or buyer many headaches. *Nick Nicaise*

Tubular steel exhaust headers led to bullet-shaped glass-pack mufflers, which in turn led to pipes exiting just ahead of the rear wheels. This turned out to be one of Shelby's less-bright ideas; fumes on some cars washed back into the open windows, it was possible to burn a shin on the hot pipes, and a few states technically didn't allow side exhausts. Toward the end of the 1965 production, cars headed for Florida, New Jersey, and California received pipes that went straight through to the back of the car. In 1966, this would be picked up across the board.

Standard throughout 1965, however, were Cobra valve covers, a finned oil pan, and a Cobra high-rise intake manifold, all in aluminum. Mounted on the manifold was a Holley 715cfm (cubic feet per minute) four-barrel carburetor featuring a center-pivot float,

Most 1966 interior parts are standard Mustang, and those that aren't—an under-dash gauge housing, high-mounted tach, and Shelby-centered wheel badge—can usually be salvaged while replacing everything else with off-the-rack Ford parts. *Nick Nicaise*

The bulk of GT350H production had special rocker stripes like this; later owners often had the cars repainted and substituted regular GT350 stripes in their place, so a black Shelby without these gold markings may well have started life as a Hertz car regardless. *Nick Nicaise*

which eliminated the stock Mustang's nasty habit of starving out in long, hard corners. (The Holley unit became hard to find parts for, and has disappeared from many GT350s after the fact. It's a valuable stock addition.) The intake and exhaust mods boosted horsepower from Ford's claimed 271 to 306 by Shelby's reckoning.

Originally the GT350 had a trunk-mounted battery to help even out the weight distribution. As production went on, these batteries turned out to be more trouble than most owners thought they were worth. Corrosion and fumes were the two big problems, and the battery was left where it was, up front in all street cars from about SFM5S335. (An interim solution was to put vented Cobra battery caps on trunk-mounted units—original and NOS batteries like this are exceedingly rare.)

Wherever the battery is located, inspect the surrounding metal closely for corrosion. Acid damage in the trunk is more common but easier to fix (it's still a pain). Very serious rust from an underhood battery—between the shock tower and firewall—can be a much more costly matter.

Around the time the first 100 street cars were completed, Shelby American finally made the big move they had been needing for a while. The old Scarab works in Venice had been getting mighty cramped with the production of Cobras, the GT40 racing program, and GT350 production all sharing the same grounds. To assemble the GT350s, in fact, mechanics brought parts and tools to the cars rather than having the cars themselves move by, production-line style, the way Henry Ford had pioneered it three generations earlier. Executive Peyton Cramer leased two huge aircraft hangars on the grounds of Los Angeles International Airport for Shelby American's new digs, and the operation moved lock, stock, and barrel in March of 1965.

With the new plant up and running, GT350s could be built faster and more cheaply, production could be increased, and the 427 Cobra and GT40 programs had room to breathe on their own again. But in another

Bowing of the fiberglass hood on early Shelbys is almost endemic—one Shelby expert, in fact, claims that an un-warped hood can almost be considered an unoriginal modification! Warping like this makes the upper surface almost impossible to align with the fenders, but that's the nature of the beast. *Nick Nicaise*

Simple, understated GT350 badge at the rear of this Hertz model reflected Shelby's desire to keep his cars tasteful. Sales figures would later prove this to be a mistake, but nowadays collectors appreciate Carroll's original point of view. Reproductions of this piece are available. *Nick Nicaise*

way, the move marked the beginning of the end for Shelby as it had been. What started as a tightly knit, almost family atmosphere began to take on the trappings of a real industrial business. Shelby American was moving away from being an upstart racing organization and into being a serious car maker. The time had come, and Shelby had proved what he set out to prove; still, some people were sad to see it go.

GT350 R-Model

Only thirty-seven GT350R cars were produced, the two prototypes already mentioned and those made in three subsequent batches. Most are accounted for as currently owned or known destroyed, but unlike many other Shelby products, there are a few that have fallen through the cracks. While this of course adds an air of excitement to the tale, it also adds much more room for forgeries—beware.

Regardless, the R-model (Shelby's factory-prepped GT350 racer) achieved what Ford and Shelby intended all along with the GT350 program. They were racetrack terrors, often

Some owners actually installed padlocks through the hood pins of their cars. That's fine for just sitting in a parking lot, but the locks can bang around and crack the hood if driven like this. *Mike Lamm*

beating the single-carb 289 Cobras that had been sent down to B-Production in 1967, and they placed the Mustang solidly in the limelight of sports car competition. A separate crew dealt with and campaigned R-models while the folks assigned to street GT350s handled the peculiar troubles of production cars.

Two of the first three white fastbacks delivered to Shelby American became R-model prototypes. When the specifications for these and the one street machine were finalized, Shelby made his order from San Jose and the ball got rolling. But fifteen of the cars from that first shipment were built differently from the rest at the Ford plant; to be exact, they were *un-built* differently.

These fifteen were made without side or rear windows, sound and heat insulation, gas tanks, interiors and headliners, and heater units. Assigned Shelby VIN numbers 094 through 108 (to drive home the fact to the SCCA that 100 cars had indeed been built for homologation), these cars were taken into a special area of the Shelby American works and prepared for pure racing duty.

Though all four groups of R-models (two prototypes and batches of fifteen, five, and fifteen cars) were built in their own series at San Jose and Shelby American, cars within these batches were taken in for preparation at random. In other words, the Ford and Shelby VINs correspond by group, but not numerically *within* each group. Regardless, the SAAC has the records under lock and key to let a buyer know if a given Ford and Shelby number pair jibe as an R-model.

The suspension work essentially already done, Shelby turned to the engines, interiors, bodies, and details of the R-models. The engines were removed, balanced, and blueprinted; heads were sent out for porting and polishing, and the manifold ports were matched to the heads on reassembly. Each engine was fitted with hefty tubular exhaust headers *sans* muffling and then run in on Shelby's dynamometer to be tuned to racing specs. Initially a target of 350hp was set, with some engines hitting as much as 360 and some falling 25 horses shy of their expectation; no matter. As each car was raced, its engine was torn down and modified to the point that power figures were all over the scale by the time the dust cleared.

Plexiglass side windows with aluminum frames saved weight, and the heavy Mustang air extractor was removed from the rear roof quarters and replaced with a simple aluminum panel. Plexiglass rear windows were installed, each one featuring a 1in beveled gap at its upper edge which ducted air out of the cockpit and smoothed the flow over the rear of the car. Dash pads were removed and six CS-logo gauges were installed in front of the driver, who sat in either a fiberglass or

Standard Mustang air extractors in the sail panels were only used on the 1965 model run. They were heavy and created a large blind spot, so the 1966 GT350's plexiglass window replacement was a big help here. *Mike Lamm*

Simple aluminum panel riveted over the former air extractor opening was a lightweight and easy solution to Shelby's weight problems on factory racers. This isn't something the average Shelby owner will do after the fact. *Mike Lamm*

stock Mustang bucket seat, depending on what Shelby had available at the time. Aluminum sheet replaced the inner door panels, and a four-point roll bar was fixed into place—these would get tested under fire on more than a few cars.

Outside the car, fenders had to be opened up and flared to accommodate 7x15in American Racing five-spoke magnesium wheels. Front fenders were flared and their edges were pounded flat, while initially the rear fenders were physically cut out before flaring and radiusing. This proved to be more trouble than it was worth—it meant rewelding the inner and outer fender wells since the factory welds were ground out in the process. So after the first five or six R-models, a less drastic cut was made and the original welds were preserved. In either case, the rear fenders were noticeably flared and flattened and the American Racing wheels sat menacingly deep inside them. This fender work is sometimes a good guide to a car's true identity.

Trunk panels were secured with one of the same Klik-pins as used on the fiberglass hoods; underneath them sat a special 34gal fuel tank. Open up the trunk and you were faced with a 3in quick-release fuel filler surrounded by a splash-protecting funnel of spun aluminum; the standard rear gas cap was eliminated and a round aluminum plate was riveted over the hole.

Sports Car Club of America rules allowed the removal of front and rear bumpers, which cut down on weight at the critical far ends of the cars. In place of the front bumper and valance panel, Shelby American mounted a fiberglass apron that jutted forward and featured a large square cutout in the center to direct air into the car's large oil cooler and Galaxie radiator. Two holes on either side of the cutout vented fresh air to the front brakes, a smallish pair on the earlier cars and a longer oval set beginning with the final batch of fifteen cars, starting at SFM5R527.

That last batch, incidentally, is often referred to as the *1966* R-models; they were assembled after regular 1965 GT350 production had shut down and featured 1966 style grilles and tape side stripes. They were given serial numbers, though, and titled as 1965 models.

The special R-model front valance was attractive enough to find its way onto a lot of "regular" GT350s in later years. Since setting things right—basically finding and installing a stock Mustang bumper and valance—will be easily offset by the value of the valance itself, don't bother taking money off for this aftermarket addition.

As Shelby American built and sold GT350 R-models the cars quickly established a winning reputation on the track. In the 1965 racing season, winning A-Production races essentially meant owning a Cobra; winning B-Production meant owning a Shelby GT350R. Five of the six SCCA B-Production regional titles were won by the cars, and the runoffs saw GT350s take first, second, fourth, sixth, seventh, ninth, and tenth places. No big shock, really, when ten of the fourteen cars entered had been GT350s. Throughout 1965, Shelby American was extremely fair and liberal about sharing information they'd learned from their own cars with privateers similarly equipped.

That was perhaps the greatest triumph of the R-model; you could drive a trailer up to

60

your local Ford dealer, load up a GT350R, and suddenly have the most competitive car on the track. There was nothing to be done, no strings to pull, and no two-jumps-ahead factory breathing down your neck. For perhaps the first time ever, a legitimate contender could be purchased right off the showroom floor.

Worth mentioning while discussing the R-models are the nine 1965 and four 1966 GT350s specially developed for drag racing. As with a run of AC-based cars called Dragonsnakes, demand for a drag car within and outside of the Shelby organization led to a limited but still successful program in that area. These cars were not built in series, so only Shelby paperwork or SAAC (Shelby American Automobile Club) records can truly identify one today. Still, the equipment on them was unusual enough to make them pretty easy to spot.

The cars originally featured Belanger dragracing headers, Cure-ride front shocks, a special Cobra scattershield, Hurst shifter, an engine torque strap, and AFX rear traction bars. Engines weren't modified by Shelby, partly to place the cars in a lower horsepower class and partly because drag racers were

1965-1966 R-Model and Drag Car Numbers

R-Model (All numbers begin SFM5R–)
Prototypes: 001, 002
First batch: 094–108
Second batch: 209–213
Third batch: 527–540
Note: One car from the last batch remains unaccounted for, and factory documents indicate that it was never, in fact, built.

Drag Cars
1965: SFM5S206, 207, 327, 360, with five serial numbers unaccounted for.
1966: SFM6S011, 021, 046, and 182.

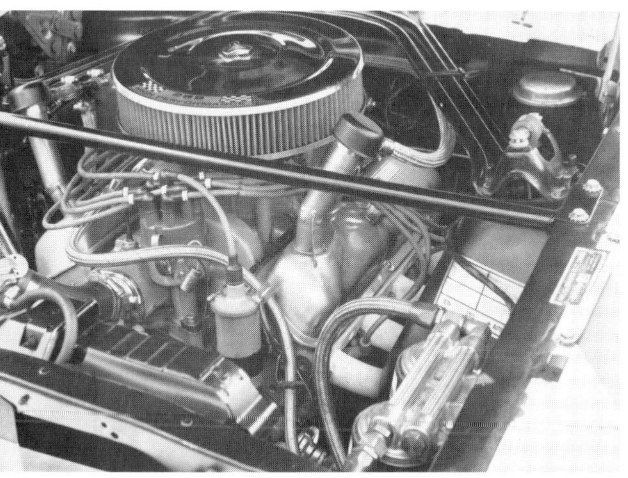

With the possible exception of all that bracing, there was nothing particularly romantic looking about the GT350R's engine bay. Racing modifications like spring-retained breather caps and dipstick, braided lines, and twin remote filters were made as racing, not fashion, dictated. *Mike Lamm*

Fading GT350 gas cap presents buyers and owners with a quandary; a repro replacement would make the whole car look sharper, but there's a certain honesty to this original's condition. Since the paint scheme isn't stock here and originality is obviously not important, a replacement is probably in order. (Save that old cap, though!) *Mike Lamm*

sure to rebuild them anyway. An added bonus was that the scattershield and heavy-duty clutch-plate assembly could be stuck in the trunk on delivery—Shelby American didn't have to pull the engine to install them beforehand.

An unrestored R-model will likely have all sorts of goofy racing equipment left over from its later life, and unfortunately this can make any old garden-variety SCCA Mustang seem at first like an R-model. Look of course for the proper ID tags, and the more expensive R-model additions like plexiglass windows with aluminum frames, the unique beveled rear window, and the steel radiused fenders.

1966 Shelby GT350

With Shelby's move to the Los Angeles airport came one striking difference in the way his company did business. Up until that time, Ford had considered Shelby American something of a small-potatoes shop. But the move to larger quarters really drove home the point that Shelby's people were no longer just an outside concern with some tenuous ties to the Ford Motor Co. They were, for better or worse, rapidly becoming one more part of the vast Ford empire, and the GT350 sealed it.

But Ford became tired, frankly, of losing money on all of Shelby's projects. While the company definitely came out ahead in the long run—through glamor rubbing off the Shelbys onto their more plebian models—it was decided to rein in some of the expenses of Shelby's outfit in hopes of cutting its costs. It was even conceivable that Shelby's Mustangs could be coaxed into turning a profit on their own.

In 1966 some inroads were made in that direction. Ford's money men took a long, hard look at the GT350: its sales, its buyer demographics, its dealer reports, and its equipment. What they found didn't surprise anyone. While an awful lot of buyers liked the *idea* of owning a street-ready race car, they were less enthusiastic about the reality of it. To some people, the very equipment that made the GT350 an uncompromising race car demanded too many owner compromises in normal use.

Dealers reported resistance to the GT350's two-seat layout, its stiff ride, loud exhaust, high price, traditional Mustang appearance, and many of its individual performance features. The Detroit Locker limited-slip differential came in for criticism time and time again—it did, admittedly, sound like a 2x4 snapping in half as it locked and unlocked under acceleration—and the manual-only transmission alienated some buyers.

At first glance, you'd think Carroll Shelby would have scoffed at these complaints; Enzo Ferrari would have, after all. But the 1965 GT350 had fulfilled the goal Shelby had set and then some; he'd already stretched a 100-plus car specialty project into more than 550 street-legal racing cars. That, realistically, wasn't too far from the saturation point of American speed loonies ready to live with a narrow-focus race car day in and day out.

A new and wider market had to be targeted, so some changes had to be made. These started appearing as a general softening of the car throughout the 1966 model year. It's fair to say most of the changes that lessened the racetrack edge of the GT350 also made it a more practical—and sometimes simply a better—car on the road. Even more importantly, however, they made the car *cost less*, which meant more profit, or actually less loss, for the manufacturer.

It should also be noted that while many performance features disappeared—things like the lowered front A-arms, drive shaft and safety loop, and the overrider traction bars—others would come to take their places, like functioning rear brake scoops, plexiglass rear quarter panes (which eliminated the large blind spot of the 1965 model), and an optional Paxton supercharger. All in all, the redirection of the GTs that began in 1966—and snowballed in the years that followed—did not make for any less of a car than the 1965 model. It made for a *different* car, in some ways better and in other ways worse.

The first 252 1966 Shelbys were virtually identical to the 1965 cars under the skin. And for good reason—they *were* 1965 models, cars that had been cranked out with some special equipment at San Jose to keep Shelby occupied while Mustang production switched over for 1966. Shelby American added 1966 cosmetics and that was that.

Even these 252 "leftover" cars had some of the less costly 1966 features. The 1965 model's dedicated instrument bezel was replaced by Ford's stock Mustang GT instrument cluster (which already had an oil pressure gauge), and a single Cobra logo tach in the center of the dash pad angled toward the driver. The steering wheel became a fake wood Mustang unit with a special GT350 cap in the center, which actually honked the horn—wonder of wonders. The much-misunderstood Detroit Locker was moved to the options list, rather than included standard, and a stock Mustang fold-down rear seat was included for the first time as an option. All but eighty-two of the 2,380 cars built that year got them, making a two-seater 1966 relatively notable. (The rear seat option cost buyers $50, a clever marketing ploy considering it cost Ford less to leave them in than to take them out.)

The first 252 cars also didn't have the mandatory-for-1966 rear back-up lights and four-way emergency flashers. Apparently, Shelby American was able to dance around the paperwork and get the cars registered regardless.

After the leftover cars were built into GT350s, Ford's economic thinking started to take hold. The most expensive modification Shelby made to a GT350 was lowering the front A-arms; from SFM6S253 on, the front A-arms were left the way they came from Ford except by rare arrangement with Shelby American. The complicated overrider traction bars also got the axe when the supply ran out around the 800th car; they were replaced with easier-to-install (but less effective) Traction Master underride bars.

The first 252 cars were all white like their predecessors, as were the first true 1966 cars. But soon a host of other colors appeared: Sapphire Blue, Candy Apple Red, Raven Black, and Ivy Green. While white cars still could receive blue Le Mans stripes, the other colors offered white Le Mans and rocker stripes. (Black Hertz cars featured gold stripes, but we'll get to those later.)

Also available for the first time was Ford's C-4 automatic transmission, something of a shock to the traditional Shelby buyer but very practical considering Ford's edict of selling more cars. These cars ran slightly detuned engines, a Ford Autolite 460 taking the place of the Holley that came on the manually

shifted cars. The fully adjustable but expensive Koni shocks also were replaced by heavy-duty Ford shock absorbers after SFM6S252. Konis could of course be added after the fact, and have been on many cars.

At first the wheel options were the same as in 1965, silver-painted steel Kelsey-Hayes 15-inchers and the optional Cragar 15in mag. But as production continued, three new wheels appeared: 14in silver-painted stamped steel units that looked almost exactly like the earlier 15-inchers; a 14in painted steel Magnum 500 (an attractive unit that looked something like an airy mag); and a unique cast-aluminum ten-spoke 14-incher.

In general, hoods were changed from steel-reinforced fiberglass to all-steel pieces around SFM6S470. They reverted back to the old fiberglass design about 450 cars later, and then the all-steel hood was brought back again for the last 150 or so cars. Don't worry about what sort of hood a given car has, just make sure it's in nice shape. Shelby changed

Some "1966" R-models ran with functional rear brake scoops while others did not. It isn't proof one way or another about a car's originality. *Mike Lamm*

For 1965, this was the biggest external indicator that you'd paid extra for a Shelby instead of a regular Mustang. In 1965 the stripes were painted and the lettering was an applique—for 1966, the entire decoration was a decal. *Mike Lamm*

the design frequently because none of them proved satisfactory.

Dealer-installed options made the GT350 even more comfortable than Shelby American's own line changes. As in 1965, a host of rear axles could be supplied by the dealer to supplement the stock 3.89:1 ratio four-speed or 3.50 automatic. Air conditioning (standard Mustang type) and a choice of radios could be installed at the dealership, and buyers could specify a real wood-rimmed wheel while they were at it.

The last six GT350s off the line were convertibles, special cars for Carroll Shelby's special friends and not initially sold to the public. Each was a different color—green, pink, white, blue, red, and yellow—and all but two were automatics. All convertibles had standard 306hp engines. The cars did, of course, eventually find their way to market— along with at the very least one known blatant copy built later. They have not all been accounted for, however. Two remain at large, with one of them reportedly having been crashed.

In 1979, Shelby decided to build another "1966" convertible GT350, a car for which he had a particularly soft spot in his heart. Shelby American contacted Beverly Hills Mustang to do the work, for which a stock Mustang convertible bodyshell was to be located and stripped, then refitted with as many original and exact reproduction GT350 parts as possible. (There were so many of these parts that an exact copy could easily be made.) Beverly Hills Mustang realized it was on to a good thing, and with Shelby's blessing the project grew from one car to a dozen. Ten were eventually built: one for Shelby and three for his family, four for customers, and three for Beverly Hills Mustang. The serial numbers of these cars picked up at SFM6S2381, exactly where 1966 GT350 production left off, although 2381 was never constructed by the time the project ended.

Whether these cars are really GT350s or not is a matter of semantics to the people who are buying and selling them. They did get Carroll Shelby's blessing and they were his creation, but they never saw the inside of a Shelby factory. As long as you know what you're buying, then it's your call.

GT350 Hertz

According to one writer, the GT350 Hertz was thus named because to rent one you had to "Pay 'till it Hertz." A full 40 percent of GT350 production went to Hertz in 1966, greatly shoring up Shelby's sales and maybe even preventing Ford from pulling the plug then and there.

Regardless, the GT350H, as it was called, was a tremendous boon for Shelby and a fascinating slice of 1960s car culture for the rest of us. Much of what is known today—the Hertz tale was based more on rumor and assumption than facts until recently—comes from the efforts of a few die-hard Shelby American Automobile Club members who really went to town on the car. Today, the story seems clear up to a point.

There were a tremendous number of running changes introduced during the GT350H run, those that affected the regular cars and more that were made on the Hertz vehicles only. The end result is that a GT350 today may or may not be a Hertz car, regardless of what it says on the rocker stripes, but the special Hertz equipment is fairly extensive. All of the legitimate Hertz VIN numbers have been documented by factory paperwork.

The story began with a feeler from Shelby American to Hertz, which had a program at the time called the Hertz Sports Car Club. Club members—older, respectable and wealthy regular renters—had the option of selecting a niftier-than-usual car from the Hertz fleet on occasion, usually a Corvette because Hertz was being supplied with General Motors cars. Shelby American suggested that the GT350 enter the program when Hertz began buying vehicles from Ford, and Hertz tentatively agreed it might be a good idea. Hertz asked for a demo car to be sent to its headquarters with special rocker stripes saying GT350H (for Hertz, of course), and Shelby obliged.

Peyton Cramer had done a little research on Hertz, and learned that its original rental cars had borne the Hertz name and a special black and brass paint scheme. The demo car, SFM6S048, was done up in these colors, the body being black of course and the rocker and Le Mans stripes being gold. Hertz mulled the idea over for a spell and, no doubt in part because black and gold looked so *good* on the GT350, ordered 100 of them.

Chromed and jointed Monte Carlo bar and Y-bracing look nifty, but unless they use the same mounting holes as the original parts they'll be a real bear to set right. Street drivers won't care nearly as much as show-car owners about this kind of thing, but this engine bay's gone perhaps a bit too far. *Nick Nicaise*

Looking at the Shelby Mustangs

In addition to items mentioned in specific chapters, the information below applies to *all* Shelby Mustangs. Most parts are standard Ford issue, and as one expert puts it, "The things that go wrong with Shelbys are pretty much the same things that go wrong with Mustangs."

Unique Shelby Pieces

Special badging, engine parts, bumpers, interior trim, suspension equipment, and fiberglass pieces are the things you can't get at the local Ford shop; ergo, these parts are usually costly. All engine and grille badges are merely relocated stock Mustang items, but emblems like the coiled snake and GT350 logo are tougher to come by. Virtually all Shelby parts are available in reproduction, but the quality varies—an expert should recommend each piece.

Rust

Cowl rust is common and can be very costly. Also common and very, *very* costly is severe rust below front-mounted batteries (this area is load-bearing and *must* be repaired). Check all rockers by tapping with the back of a screwdriver—if rust rains down inside, expensive rocker replacements are necessary. Floorboards and trunk floors commonly rust, and replacement is relatively cheap only as long as sound metal exists at all four corners, allowing new sections to be welded in. Rust around wheelwells is common; front fender rust on the outer panel only is a minor repair; outer rear fender rust is more costly but not prohibitive; rust that extends to either inner fender (which is usually the case) at least doubles the cost of the repair. Frame rail stampings *must* be solid or pricey repairs will be needed. Minor door pillar, rear window surround, or windshield area rust is a mid-level repair; extensive rust in these locations can be very costly.

Doors

Mustang doors are poorly rustproofed on the inside so rot is common, especially at the bottoms—the best repair is often a complete and inexpensive door swap with salvaged Mustang parts. Lower hinges are notoriously weak and most doors sag after 50,000 miles; replacing the hinges is a simple fix. At about the same age, doors become hard to close and/or unlatch from the inside, caused by the latches sinking into the door posts; a very minor repair if rust hasn't attacked the weakened door post metal.

Interiors

All parts but unique Shelby gauges, consoles, seats, belts, badges, and rollbars are standard Mustang items and are readily available on the aftermarket. Cracked dashboards and torn headliners are time-consuming repairs but the parts, at least, are inexpensive; abused carpeting, seats, and door panels are cheap and easy to fix. Windshields and rear windows are readily available, side glass a little less so, and convertible side glass can be downright difficult to find. Weatherstripping rots quickly, allowing moisture and rust in the interior—the weatherstripping itself is inexpensive, the resulting damage often less so. Windshield and rear window leaks are common; the only acceptable repair is fully removing the glass and resealing the joint—beware of goop slapped on after the fact.

Engines

Shelby drivetrains are generally quite robust. Hi-Po 289, 428 Police Interceptor, and 390 rebuilds are reasonable; 302 and 351 rebuilds are very reasonable; 428 CJ and 427 rebuilds can be costly. (Some evidence indicates 428 CJ engines routinely last less than 100,000 miles between rebuilds.) Proper Holley 715cfm carbs are rare and costly. Most other intake and exhaust parts are readily available through Mustang or Shelby suppliers.

Drivelines

Aluminum-case Borg-Warner transmissions are exceedingly costly, all others are reasonably priced. Clutches present few problems. Detroit Locker and Traction-Lok rear ends can be expensive to repair but are essentially strong; noisy operation on lockup is normal. Ford limited-slip units are reasonably priced as used parts.

Suspension and Brakes

Replacing unique Shelby suspension pieces like Pitman and idler arms, override traction bars, and stiffer springs can cost good money, but most suspension work is reasonably priced. All braking systems except competition-spec aluminum systems and the 1966 GT350H MICO brake booster are straightforward and inexpensive.

Shelby introduced what would become their trade-mark ten-spoke aluminum wheel in 1966, a very valuable option. Fitted to the 1966 cars should be the 14in variety, not the more common 15-incher brought out for 1967. *Nick Nicaise*

One hundred cars was already more than Shelby American had expected, but more were quickly ordered: first another batch of 100 and then, after the initial response started coming in from Hertz's advertising and PR people, 800 more cars for a grand total of 1,000. The first 200 were to be black and gold, and at the same time Shelby American was asked to supply an automatic-equipped car for evaluation.

The automatic quickly became Hertz's transmission of choice; 85 of the first 100 Hertz cars actually made it out the hangar door with a four-speed. The remaining 800 cars from the final order were originally to be a mix of all the Shelby colors, but after about 230 non-black cars were produced (some without Le Mans stripes) Hertz decided to go back to the black and gold paint scheme and stick with it. In other words, about three out of four of the final production cars got the distinctive black and gold treatment.

All Hertz cars received radios in production (of different varieties but mostly Motorolas), and all, apparently, had a fender-mounted antenna. Most also had special manual brake boosters, a by-product of renters who were unfamiliar with hard competition brake linings. The semi-metallic linings originally used were quite fade-resistant when hot, but also rather *stop*-resistant when cold. This meant the driver had to put a stiff boot in to get the car to slow, and Hertz received complaints from more than a few rather alarmed drivers.

The solution came in two areas, a MICO piggyback brake booster (a troublesome unit that's been replaced on most cars with a standard Ford master cylinder) and a warning decal on the dashboard of the car. The decal, bordered by checkered flags, read "This vehicle equipped with competition brakes. Heavier than normal brake pedal pressure may be required." Not only did that clear Hertz of any responsibility, it made renters feel like they were getting their $17 a day and seventeen cents a mile's worth.

Other unique features are more likely to still be on these cars. The speedometer had a special tamper-proof cable junction to prevent it from being disconnected from the speedo head. The master cylinder mounting bracket on most Hertz cars was of course unique (it allowed a three-bolt master cylinder to be put onto the two-bolt master cylinder location), and wheels were 14x6in chrome Magnum 500s from Motor Wheel and featured chrome lugs.

Stories abound about the adventures of various Hertz cars, some of them no doubt apocryphal. A favorite tale has long been told about "a friend of a friend" who worked at Hertz, and one Monday he found weld marks under the carpets where somebody had rented the car, installed a roll bar, raced it and then removed the bar and brought it back. Maybe, maybe not. Since most Hertz cars were automatics with the smallish Autolite carburetor, it's likely the vast majority were used for their intended purpose—fast street driving—and little else. Yet long-time SAAC members report that they either rented the cars to drag race on Sundays, or remember seeing them race.

The Shelby/Hertz relationship didn't end with the 1,000 unit run of 1966 models. In 1968 and 1969, Hertz ordered more GT350s, this time apparently all with automatic transmissions. These cars featured no Hertz-specific goodies, though—no special badges, paint schemes, or braking systems— and no heavy advertising campaign was associated with them. If documentation exists to show a particular 1968 (shown here) or 1969 GT350 began its career in the Hertz fleet, it gives the car some entertaining history but shouldn't affect its value one way or the other. It's the 1966 cars people remember. *Hertz, courtesy Michael Dregni*

Chapter 6

1967-1968 Shelby

1967 GT350:	7.5
1967 GT500:	7.5
1968 GT350:	7
1968 GT500:	7.5
1968 GT350 convertible:	7.5
1968 GT500 convertible:	8
1968 GT500KR:	8
1968 GT500KR convertible:	8.5

1967 Shelby

Shelby American and Ford Motor Co. took heed of the lesson they had learned in 1966; as more usable interior space and fewer costly race-bred pieces were put on the Shelby Mustang, the car's sales grew considerably. GT350 production for 1966 ran more than four times that of the year before, admittedly with help from Hertz' 1,000 unit order; in any case, it was quite an improvement. The more road-ready Shelbys were proving far better sellers than the race-inspired vehicles.

One complaint that still surfaced frequently, however, was the consumer's reluctance to shell out considerably more money for a car that still looked so much like a stock Mustang. Shelby and Ford realized it would be wise to spend more money on the exterior where people could see it, rather than on the

Stretched 1968 nose with those angry eyebrows over the headlights radically changed the Shelby's looks; the fiberglass pieces can be pretty spotty, however, which is just the nature of the beast. A good fiberglass shop can rework them into near perfection, but Shelby American rarely did. *Nick Nicaise*

The 1968 Shelby wheel covers harken back to earlier Cragar magnesium wheels, but they didn't fool anyone. There's nothing wrong with them, but of course aluminum Shelby wheels will add more value to the car. Very fastidious owners will have saved the original wheels and covers after such a switch—their trading value is considerable.

interior where they often complained about the modifications anyway.

Considering what happened to the base Mustang in 1967, it was just as well. The car grew in length, width and somewhat in weight, and the Shelby that would be built off of its platform had to be larger and heavier as well. The upsizing, which might have been anathema to Shelby's thinking of just a couple of years earlier, did allow for one very nifty payoff: the Mustang's engine bay was suddenly wide enough to accept a big-block Ford engine.

With America's tastes running more and more toward comfort and straight-line acceleration, a 1967 Shelby big-block would be just the ticket. Of course, the emphasis on straight-line speed has led to many of these cars getting flogged throughout their lives, so today you need to give the entire driveline a good check for signs of abuse.

Despite the general softening of the platform, the 1967 Shelby was still a performance car of considerable merit, ready, willing and able to take on upstarts from Chevrolet and Pontiac in the pony and muscle car field.

Though a larger share of the development cash was being put into the looks of the car this year, the underpinnings would still be special.

While the original GT350 had undergone major suspension surgery in Shelby's cramped Venice, California, shop, the 1967 Shelbys got a standard heavy-duty Mustang suspension before they rolled down the line at the Los Angeles International Airport plant. Shelby being Shelby, of course, a few modifications had to be made. Unique-to-Shelby variable-rate front springs were added, with overall ratings of 330psi (pounds per square inch) for 289 engined cars and 365psi on the 428s. (The effective rate of the spring increased as the unit was compressed, due to different winding lengths of the coils.) A larger-than-stock (but smaller than before) front antiroll bar was put on the car, 0.94in in diameter, to control the body roll that the larger Mustang platform would inevitably experience.

Knowing a good thing when he saw it, Shelby retained the export brace to stiffen up the front end of the car. The Monte Carlo bar disappeared, however, not deemed worth the trouble for a car that would see little if any track time. The common aftermarket bar tying the shock towers together certainly won't hurt anything except, perhaps, the car's value. Make sure there aren't any tough-to-repair holes drilled in the engine bay to mount the piece, and see if the bar will make distributor or carburetor work difficult.

Adjustable Gabriel shocks became the only ones available, the costly Koni option being dropped, and simple rubber axle stops replaced the traction bars of earlier Shelbys— something that would definitely be missed. Ugly aftermarket ladder bars are a common addition, and again watch out for permanently drilled mountings.

The relative lack of suspension modification reflected a new and cost-efficient outlook at Shelby, but it also reflected something else: the Ford boys were starting to get a handle on the Mustang's handling. If the 1967 Shelby didn't receive the suspension tweaking of its predecessors, one big reason was simply that the stock heavy-duty Mustang pieces worked so well to begin with.

Under the hood of the GT350, cast-iron Ford exhaust manifolds replaced the tubular headers on earlier cars. (Another common replacement site, naturally.) Shelby still rated the engine at 306bhp, which could mean a few things: either the old-style headers weren't actually doing anything for the car (unlikely), extra horsepower was picked up from another location (also unlikely, as the rest of the engine was virtually identical from 1966 to 1967), or there was a little license taken in the advertising (bet on it!). It's entirely possible that both engines actually dynoed above 306hp, the 1967 unit just a little bit less. (These stats, of course, relate only to manually shifted cars with their Holley 715cfm carburetor. The automatics "made do" with a Ford Autolite 595cfm four-barrel piece, and their peak output was off just a bit. Either carb should still be in place; an aftermarket carburetor that's poorly tuned to the engine can be asking for trouble.)

As good an engine as the 289 remained, the big news was in the new Shelby model: for another $200, buyers could opt for the GT500. The year 1967 saw America in the throes of a big-cubes, big-power battle, and Shelby responded by sticking a 428ci Police Interceptor V-8 into the Shelby bodyshell to create an all-new animal. The hydraulic-lifter

Molded plastic covering on roll bar of convertibles made them more palatable to the fashion-minded. The covering can get chewed up in the sun, so look for fading and cracks. Sound replacements can be a real bear to come by.

A Shelby's panel fit won't always be the greatest, due to fiberglass supplier problems. The hoodline is off here, but a lot of other Shelbys share this problem. Don't let it bother you too much on anything but an intended show car. *Nick Nicaise*

The 1968's rear spoiler and valance can be hard to come by. The antenna mast is normally, but not exclusively, in this position on Coupes—front fender mounting is also seen on occasion. *Nick Nicaise*

428 was no match for the more exotic 427 from which Shelby built his racing engines, but—as with the 427 Cobra—it had more than enough power to get the job done on the street. At first, two four-barrel Holley 650cfm carbs sat on an aluminum medium-rise intake manifold, providing up to 1,300cfm of air to be mixed with great swigs of gasoline in producing a rated 355hp. (That figure was, oh, a *wee tad* conservative.)

Topping off the engine were the now-familiar Cobra valve covers along with an attractive oblong aluminum air cleaner case. On early cars this case is simply ribbed, but soon the word Cobra appeared here as well. A very small number of GT500s were rumored to have received the more exotic 427 medium-riser engine, which was listed as an option. A critical eye should be given to any car so advertised. They certainly do exist, but there's a great deal of doubt that any of these cars got the 427 at the factory. For these vehicles, documentation from the factory or dealer is everything; so far, none have reliably shown up with the proper W engine code they would normally have received.

The GT350 and GT500 had very different personalities, and one cannot be assumed to be better than the other. Most dealers, of course, liked to give the impression that since the larger engine cost more money, you got more car. What you actually got was more power and more straight-line speed in exchange for more overall weight, and particularly more weight in the nose. (The engine and bellhousing alone accounted for nearly 170lb extra. Add in heavier springs, mounts, automatic transmissions, and so on, and the numbers do creep up.)

The GT350 was still an excellent-handling automobile, while the GT500 gave up quite a bit in the corners for the sake of really moving on the straights. Wise buyers chose the model they wanted for the sort of use they'd give it, but a number of customers simply bought into the "more is better" thinking and opted

The Police Interceptor 428—or maybe it's a 390, you'll never know without tearing the engine apart—pretty much filled up the 1968's engine bay. The bent Monte Carlo bar is an aftermarket addition, since Shelby dropped these pieces in 1967. Unlike many other Shelbys, this engine package really looked the part of a hot rod. *Nick Nicaise*

The 1968's rather uninspired Mustang interior and steering wheel detracts from an otherwise visually enjoyable package. Center console, unique to Shelby, carries ancillary gauges and can be a tough replacement. *Nick Nicaise*

for the GT500 if they had the extra cash. The GT350 wound up accounting for 1,175 of the 3,225 Shelbys built that year. It's doubtful that anyone was disappointed either way they went, and there's surprisingly little price difference between the two today.

All 1967 Shelbys apparently got power brakes and steering (and buyers were dinned accordingly to the tune of $200, like it or not). Despite the cost, the power assists were generally liked by buyers and roundly hated by automotive journalists. (The SAAC does report that a few cars might have originally been fitted with manual steering.) An automatic transmission (C-6 for the GT500 and C-4 in the GT350) was offered for $50 extra, along with Ford top-loader four-speeds in either model. The shift linkage on both transmissions can get sloppy over time, but the fix is usually a simple bushing swap.

The GT500's manual transmission featured a heavier output shaft than the GT350's. Again the Paxton supercharger was offered as an option at $549, although it voided much of the factory powertrain warranty. The Detroit Locker limited-slip differential was a special order item from Shelby American,

and was a dealer-installed option. A Ford limited-slip diff could also be ordered from the dealer or by special order from Shelby in combination with a 3.50 or 4.11:1 rear-axle ratio.

The interiors were basically stock Deluxe Mustang GT in black or parchment (tan in 1968 only), and on very rare occasions white. Included was a functioning roll bar which was welded to the floor pan and bolted to the roof. A wood-rim steering wheel was carried over as a nicety, with a plastic horn button carrying Shelby's nifty new coiled-snake logo and GT350 or GT500 identification, and drivers received a remote outside mirror gratis. A fold-down rear seat was included because Shelby ordered the cars with the GT package. Today it's a handy addition to have.

A 140mph speedometer shared duty with a tachometer that (rather optimistically) read to 8000rpm. Under the center of the dash sat a set of Stewart-Warner gauges for oil pressure and amps; the gauge housing was actually a Mustang Rally-Pac cluster from 1966 that had been mounted upside down. Air conditioning and the attendant mandatory tinted glass added a rather hefty $386 to the tab.

For the first time the standard Shelby wheel was a steel unit with a wheel cover—15in Ford and recapped 1967 Thunderbird, respectively. Optional on early cars was a 15x7in Kelsey-Hayes aluminum and chrome modular wheel, and on later cars a cast-aluminum Shelby ten-spoke 15-incher. More colors came on line as the car reached out for new buyers; three different shades of blue and one each of red, white, dark green, black, metallic silver, and metallic "lime gold." Rally stripes were an unpopular dealer-installed option, in blue on white cars and white on all others.

The 289 engine was still dynamite—it had been well developed and didn't need much attention come 1967—and the 428 was an agreeable and understressed lump that didn't take much rocket science to outfit for Shelby's needs. A 1967 Shelby GT350 devoid of heavy options was still a pretty good match for a 1965 GT350 in back-road duels, while the GT500 would absolutely walk away from the earlier cars in stoplight drags. But as mentioned earlier, the bulk of Shelby's effort for 1967 went into cosmetics; the body would be

Shelby-specific ten-spoke wheels are worth a fair amount of money against the imitation-mag wheel cover also used in 1968. 1967 Shelbys used a similar 15in ten-spoker, but the two years' wheels won't interchange; slightly different machining causes the 1968 wheels to interfere with the 1967 suspension. *Nick Nicaise*

Simple GT500 rocker nomenclature marks this as an early, Police Interceptor equipped car. When the Cobra Jet engine came on line the designation was switched to GT500KR. *Nick Nicaise*

noticeably different than that of a stock Mustang, which Ford figured would attract buyers and bring more attention to the work that Shelby was doing.

As before, semi-complete cars were ordered from San Jose and shipped to Los Angeles, but for 1967 they came without hoods, headlight caps, or decks. Ford had sent a skeleton crew of designers to Los Angeles to oversee the body modifications of the 1967 Shelby, and they'd come up with a few themes.

First, by making the hood and headlight caps 3in longer than normal, the entire front end of the car could be extended to look meaner and more purposeful. Second, a prominent air scoop would be added to the roof's sail panels to extract cockpit air and generally grab attention. A side scoop was again included behind the door's trailing edge to duct cool air to the rear brakes; at first this was functional, but at some point—even the experts aren't quite sure when—they became dummies and the rear brakes had to go it alone. And third, the deck and rear end featured a prominent spoiler, a flat rear

taillight panel, and taillights which were 1967 Cougar units in '67 and NOS 1965 Thunderbird parts in 1968.

All of the special body panels would be made of fiberglass, since tooling up to build hoods, nose pieces, and decks in steel would have been prohibitive for the number of cars Shelby was building. Unfortunately, everybody knew that the quality of plastic panels wouldn't be as good as ones made of metal; Shelby American had no idea, however, just how bad some of those fiberglass pieces would be.

Finding a reliable supplier of quality fiberglass panels in southern California had already proven difficult, and with the multitude of plastic parts on the 1967 model that nuisance would become a crisis. Hoods, scoops, and decks all arrived at one time or

Close-set eyes of the early 1967 Shelbys ran afoul of some state laws, so later cars and all those heading for the offended localities went to outboard lights. The earliest cars also used body-color trim rings around the headlights instead of the chrome type shown here. Neither style should affect the car's value. *Mike Lamm*

another with problems in finish, smoothness, strength, and most of all fit.

In addition to the questionable quality of the pieces that were supplied, the original specs for those pieces were probably not very accurate, either. Before production started, Ford had sent Shelby a 1967 bodyshell to work with as a buck for the new fiberglass parts; unfortunately, they sent a car that had already been destroyed in safety testing. Shelby's people—and the Ford people under his thumb—were working by guess and by golly on the actual measurements of how the car *should* have looked before it was wrecked.

Once production started on the 1967 line in Los Angeles, it became obvious that many of the fiberglass components were way off spec. Shelby employees would eventually have to go out to the post-production line with sandpaper in hand and shape many of the pieces one by one (a contributing factor to Shelby American's eventual demise). Ill-fitting fiberglass was normal when the cars were new, but today's standards are higher. Gross panel

gaps will definitely lower a car's value, despite the fact that that's probably how it came from the factory.

The 1967 Shelby's designers played with a few details that would eventually get them into the same sort of trouble that 1965's side exhausts did. Initially, the high-beam lamps were grouped right in the middle of the grille, providing buyers with one more styling cue to separate their cars from run-of-the-mill Mustangs. Red running lights were also placed at the trailing end of the cockpit ventilation scoops. Both of these ran afoul of California's (and no doubt other states') vehicle codes, and after the first 200 cars the running lights were deleted outright while preparations were made to move the high-beams to the outboard ends of the grilles. (This took quite a bit longer, and the interim solution was simply to not send any inboard-light cars to California dealers.)

In retrospect, it's funny that the California Department of Motor Vehicles objected to those red running lights—they were wired to go on with the brake lights, much like the center high-mounted stop lamp that became mandatory equipment in the 1980s. In another instance of Shelby playing the unlikely predictor of federal safety regulations, the 1967 model featured the first use anywhere of inertial-reel shoulder harnesses. Now recognized as one of the great contributions to highway safety, these were patterned after Air Force hardware and bolted to the mandatory integral roll bar—which, of course, was *another* Shelby safety first. The inertial belt units, if they're bad, can be a bear to locate and replace, so check them out well.

As the 1967 production run was just getting under way in late 1966, Ford decided to send a few more of its people out to California to help—or possibly to keep an eye on—Shelby and his operation. Ford's involvement with Shelby had been steadily increasing, and as the production numbers grew so did the home office's interest in Shelby American's affairs.

What Ford's people found was an operation that was trying to build 3,500 cars the same way it had built 350. The production line was essentially in place, but it could stand a lot of streamlining. There was far too much handwork being done—especially with the fiberglass—for Ford's tastes, and there were considerable duplications of effort. As ominous as it sounded, Ford was right; Shelby American was building cars with soul, but there was an awful lot of monkey business going on as well. Shelby simply didn't have six decades of auto production experience to draw from; Ford did.

An array of running changes in addition to those already discussed during 1967 underscored Shelby's rather haphazard production style. Seats went from those with smooth faces to units using comfort-weave inserts; steel reinforcements disappeared once more from the hood (and now the fiberglass deck, too); four-point roll bars were replaced with simpler two-point bars after the first thirty or so cars; grilles went from one-piece to two-piece backings; fuel lines were rerouted from the transmission tunnel to the rockers; rear valances went from stock Mustang with exhaust cutouts to standard Mustang GT units; and more. It was exactly the sort of thing that would irk a production-minded executive who strived for efficiency.

After 1967 production had been tamed as best as possible, what eventually transpired was the decision to move Shelby's car-building arm to Michigan for the 1968 production run. It was a combination of many factors that led to the decision. Shelby's airport factory in Los Angeles had run out its lease and, not being directly related to airport business, seemed unlikely to get a renewal. (Besides, production would again be increased for 1968 and more room would be needed in any case.) Reliable fiberglass suppliers were hard to find on the West Coast. And finally, Ford officials admitted to themselves what they had probably suspected ever since the GT350 proved to be a viable product: They could build the car themselves for less than it cost Shelby to do it for them.

Shelby American was cut up. The main arm (as far as Ford was concerned) would move to Michigan to produce cars under the name of Shelby Automotive, Inc. The aftermarket and

Snap-on 1967 gas cap is one of those pieces that can really be a pain to replace. The caps are clear plastic with painted backs, however, and sometimes they can be brought back from the dead by a talented painter. *Mike Lamm*

Shelby introduced hood pins to the production market, although by the time 1967 rolled around they were just for show. The tremendous panel gap between hood and fender here is not at all uncommon. *Mike Lamm*

Both of these 1967 scoops show some of Shelby's trouble with fiberglass; the lower one has been chipped by stones and the upper fits very poorly against the sail panel at its leading edge. *Mike Lamm*

parts operation—Shelby Parts and Accessories—would stay out west, but as a separate legal entity from Shelby Racing, a group whose name was self-explanatory.

The changes had been inevitable, perhaps, since Shelby American grew from an upstart racing outfit into a volume manufacturer. It was only Carroll Shelby's great ability to choose good people and selflessly delegate authority that had kept it all together this far. But the empire, finally, had gotten too big to stay together.

1968 Shelby

Shelby Automotive, Inc., set up office operations in Livonia, Michigan, toward the end of 1967. The actual production of automobiles was contracted out to the A. O. Smith Company of nearby Ionia, a respected firm with experience in volume fiberglass work. (The company had already contracted out pieces for General Motors.) Ford's advertising and PR people also got to wield an even heavier hand than before, resulting in the official naming of the Shelby, which had previously been called just about whatever a dealer, owner, or writer felt like: It was now the Shelby Mustang Cobra GT350, 500, or 500KR (for King of the Road).

The method of production for 1968 was changed considerably. First, the Mustang skeletons were built in Metuchen, New Jersey, instead of San Jose. So starting in 1968, a Shelby's Ford VIN will carry a T build code (for Metuchen) instead of the R (for San Jose) used earlier. An incorrect build code means a fake Shelby, guaranteed.

In the interest of efficiency, the mechanical changes separating Shelbys from stock Mustangs were actually done on the line, rather than after the fact (everything but the relatively simple addition of carbs and intake manifolds).

Taking advantage of the low tooling costs for fiberglass, the plastic pieces of the Shelby were again redesigned for 1968. The nose came in for the most treatment: the grille opening was enlarged and became more of a one-mouth affair than before, while the headlight caps became more pointed with meaner-looking eyebrows. Twin high-intensity rectangular driving lights were mounted above the bumper at the outboard edges of the grille, and this time Shelby knew enough to clear it with the law beforehand. (The inclusion of high-visibility driving lights as standard equipment was *still another* Shelby safety first.) The hood was all new, with two wide and low scoops at its forward edge, "SHELBY" in chrome lettering across the front lip (which falls off and is a trial to find), and heat-removing (to say nothing of darned attractive) louvers at the back. Shelby's coiled-snake logo was added to the front fenders and the dash.

The tail also got revised: the rear spoiler was remodeled to give it a more pronounced center kickup, "SHELBY" lettering graced the horizontal surface, and the rear panel was contoured around NOS 1965 Thunderbird sequential turn signals and a unique Shelby snap-on gas cap (often missing, thanks to souvenir hunters). The stock wheel was again a steel Ford unit with a wheel cover, this time a five-spoker simulating the Cragar wheel on the GT350 of 1965. Unique Shelby ten-spoke aluminum wheels again were available at extra cost.

The interior was still pirated from the regular Mustang GT Deluxe package in black or tan, with a roll bar mandatory. The Rally-Pac underdash gauge housing was dropped in favor of a center console featuring two Stewart-Warner gauges (still for oil pressure and amps) in 1968, and a padded center armrest with a coiled snake embossed into the vinyl. Unique to 1968 Shelbys, the easily damaged center console is one thing you'll pay a lot to replace. A tilt steering wheel was available as an option for the first time, occasionally a mandatory one, at around $62. Today, it adds a little value to the car.

The availability of performance options was cut back for 1968, their popularity noticeably waning in 1967. In their place, dealers were encouraged to consult the Shelby Parts and Accessories catalog and equip cars with special goodies by themselves. This did two things: it made the cars cheaper and easier to produce, and it made for a rather confusing array of equipment that can still be regarded as correct "as delivered."

Everything from Shelby-style suspension components, shocks, and engine parts to interior dress-up goodies like shift knobs and fancy badges were available through the dealer before delivery. Shelbys were rarely loaded down from the parts book, but incongruous equipment on *any* car is not necessarily an owner-installed hash. It pays to get familiar with that year's parts books before making a judgment call. Some paper ferreting

Since there's no running light at the back of the upper brake scoop, this 1967 Shelby was built after the first 200 or so cars.

at the original dealer, if possible, may also prove helpful.

The standard engine in the GT350 became Ford's 302 V-8, which was definitely a disappointment to Shelby fans. While the 302 was technically a stroked-up 289, its true history split with the high-performance engine long before Shelby stirred in his witches' brew. The 302 had hydraulic lifters—which limited the revs but made for a quieter and less maintenance-intensive engine—and weaker internals than the hot 289. Even with a Shelby intake manifold and 600cfm Holley, the new engine put out a rated horsepower of just 250, quite a drop from the year before. Torque ratings were down as well, though only by about 20lb-ft. The 302s in 1968 Shelbys have often been well used as hot-shoe owners tried to wring every ounce of power from them, so check these engines out well.

An oval Cobra air cleaner case and Cobra valve covers again dressed up the smaller engine, but two available options on the 5.0 liter powerplant helped it get someplace. One was cold-air induction, which fed a denser charge to the carburetor and resulted in mildly improved performance. The other

was again a Paxton supercharger, which kicked things up to a decidedly unmild 335hp. That put the engine on par, at least as far as *rated* horsepower, with many of Ford's 7.0 liter engines. Regardless of how ratings shenanigans might obscure the true performance of all these engines, a supercharged GT350 would be undeniably strong —very rare, but strong.

On the standard 302 equipped cars, Ford countered the lowered output with a 3.89:1 rear end or a 4.11 at no extra charge. The automatic, always a poor relation in out-and-out acceleration, made do with a 3.50:1 gearset. The perennially maligned Detroit Locker could again be ordered, this time only with the 4.11 or very high 4.33 rear end. An almost-as-noisy Traction-Lok diff could be ordered for any GT350 or GT500.

Talk had originally centered on equipping the GT350 with Ford's new 351 V-8, later variations of which would go on to glory in Mustangs, Panteras, and other cars. The 351 didn't offer enough power to justify its cost, though, so the 302 was in. Ultimately, that choice didn't affect most Shelby buyers, as Ford had suspected it wouldn't. Of 4,450 1968 Shelbys, only 1,657 cars were built with the small-block engine.

The rest of the run had a big-block. Originally the engine was again the 428 Police Interceptor with hydraulic lifters, but some 390s—externally identical to the 428s and unbeknownst even to dealers—were slipped in during a 428 shortage at least once. The 428 was listed at 360hp despite its single 735cfm Holley, and again it's likely that both this engine (and the 2x4 that preceded it) handily beat out the advertised ratings.

The hot 427 also appeared in some GT500s, listed for hydraulic lifters and 400hp, but how many of these engines came out of the factory and how is a mystery. It's almost assumed that these rare cars all have dealer- or owner-installed engines; again, if you find a W engine code on the ID, the SAAC wants to hear from you.

Midway through the year Shelby announced the GT500KR, which rendered the 427 something of a moot point. Not an option on the GT500 as many people believed, the KR was actually a replacement model. It was

The combination of tall fender peaks and enveloping rear spoiler gave later Shelbys two little puddle collectors at the back of the car. Open the trunk and make sure that the weatherstripping and drain channels are working; if not, rust will follow shortly. *Mike Lamm*

only sold briefly in conjunction with the standard car, and that was while old parts—and old cars—were being used up. After that, it was the 350, 500KR, or nothing.

The KR featured Ford's Cobra Jet (CJ) engine, a powerplant that wasn't dreamed up by Shelby but followed a lot of his previous thinking. New heads with huge combustion chambers replaced those from the Police Interceptor; dished alloy pistons rode on strong connecting rods attached to a nodular-iron crank. Compression was 10.6:1, and the entire block was cast from higher-nodular iron. Topped with a single Holley 735cfm four-barrel and mandatory cold-air hood, the engine was factory-rated at 335hp—no doubt to tears of helpless mirth from Ford, which was lying through its teeth so buyers could find auto insurance. True output was in the neighborhood of more than 400hp. Under the hood, the fastest way to identify a Cobra Jet engine is the exhaust manifold bolts: regular 428s use two bolts around each port while Cobra Jets have four. You could also check the engine ID tag if you're really dedicated; CJ tags will read 418S through 421S.

Relatively docile at low revs, once the tach swung past 2000 the Cobra Jet let out a roar and leapt forward like a cat whose tail had been stepped on. Larger rear brakes had to be added to keep up with the engine, and four-speed cars got staggered rear shocks to combat the vicious axle hop the CJ engine could cause. A manual-shift 500KR without staggered shocks means something's wrong, most likely an auto-to-manual gearbox swap. Some people feel the CJ engine has proven less than bulletproof, probably due to the hard use it was bound to get. Frequent rebuilds have been reported, so give a CJ the usual thorough check. Be particularly wary of water or filings in the oil, and poor compression readings.

A host of high-performance goodies could be ordered for the Cobra Jet, everything from high-compression head kits to adjustable rockers. Drag racers flocked to the Cobra Jet engine and found it most amenable to modification—a task in which Shelby Parts and Accessories would be only too happy to assist. A GT500KR with good tires, a numer-ically high rear end, and a limited-slip differential could outrun a Ferrari 275 at the drag strip.

Besides the 500KR with Cobra Jet engine, the other big news in 1968 was the availability of a convertible Shelby for the first time to the general public. Featuring an exposed roll bar covered in attractively sculpted plastic, the cars were popular but not as successful as one would imagine—especially considering that ordering a ragtop only added $100-200 to the price tag. All told, 1,124 GT350, 500 and 500KR convertibles came off the line in 1968. Quite naturally, these cars are highly prized today; they offer all the thrills of a Shelby along with the wind in your hair, and to those who can afford them they're tremendous automobiles. The electric top was available in white or black, and a glass rear window eliminated the scratching and yellowing of other convertibles' plastic windows. Convertible Shelbys have traditionally had a tremendously high theft rate; that's not so much of a problem now that the cars are valuable enough to spend less time unattended in parking lots, but watch for fishy deals regardless.

Convertibles and coupes came in another bumper crop of hues. Metallics—dark green,

The 1967 headlight caps are actually one complete unit, which makes repairing any flaws even more costly than it would be otherwise. As with any fiberglass Shelby parts, this should be inspected very carefully for damage. *Mike Lamm*

Now manufactured in Michigan, Shelbys went to more shapely 1965 new old stock Thunderbird taillights for 1968 (1967's were pirated from the current Thunderbird). Available for a small fortune from some Shelby specialists, the same plastic units can be found at a Ford salvage yard for next to nothing. *Nick Nicaise*

lime green, medium blue, and gold—ruled the roost with red, white, black, and a rare orange or yellow filling out the line-up. Rocker stripes of course still denoted the car's engine through 350, 500, or 500KR nomenclature, but Le Mans stripes disappeared from the roster.

Running changes for 1968 were relatively minor, reflecting Ford's desire to keep costs down; in other words, they decided to do it once and do it right. Primarily, the running changes consisted of replacing the original Marchal driving lights with Lucas units (watch out for parts store cheapies) and changing the original cast-iron intake manifold over to an aluminum unit. (The iron manifolds were originally needed because the aluminum-equipped engine couldn't be emissions-tested in time for production.) In both cases, the typically un-Shelby response of a recall-and-refit order went out, but of course not all owners (or even all dealers) responded; some Lucas and/or iron-manifold cars did make it out the door. There was also a minor change made to the lower side scoop, the addition of a small character line at its front edge. This occurred at an indeterminate point of production, probably as the result of a supplier change.

Finally, somewhere in the vicinity of the 1,000th car off the line the Shelby ID plates changed from "Shelby American, Inc." to "Shelby Automotive." Presumably, this was one more example of using up old stocks before starting in with a new item.

As 1968 drew to a close, the change in the Shelby Mustang Cobras was virtually complete. More than 10,000 units had come off the line since 1965, quite a jump from the 100 homologation specials that Shelby and Ford originally planned on. In that time the car had gone from a racetrack refugee to a comfortable—if still proudly uncouth—high-speed tourer. Ford was running the show now, and not only was the Shelby different, the market was different as well.

Why was Ford continuing with the Shelby Mustang Cobra now? Production was still

This Shelby Parts and Accessories ad ran in March 1968 automotive magazines to promote "Big Stuff for Big Ford Engines." Among the items featured were the Shelby "Sidewinder" induction system, "tuned" headers, a Le Mans Kinetic Superflow solid lifter camshaft kit, valve covers and drag racing cylinder heads. The prices were attractive, especially by today's standards. This induction system, complete with carburetor and manifold, sold for $230, and the headers cost $140. *Michael Dregni*

accounting for only the smallest burp in Ford's overall appetite, so the car's sales alone probably didn't justify the trouble. The main reason to build Shelbys was still image, but Ford had its own image builders coming on line now, the Boss Mustangs, the Mach 1, and the possibility of a mid-engined exotic from Lee Iacocca's pal Alejandro De Tomaso. The Cobra and GT40 had also done their jobs, and nobody believed Ford couldn't build performance anymore. Why, then, go on?

As much as anything, it was a too-much-is-never-enough attitude at Ford that kept the Shelby Mustang Cobra program alive into 1969 and early 1970. Yes, Ford realized, it didn't *have* to stay with it, but Ford was a performance company and the Shelby was a performance product. Ford knew that in the end, it could always justify selling Shelbys simply because they couldn't put a price tag on the name.

It was Shelby who would finally pull the plug.

The pair of rectangular driving lights recessed into the grille of the 1968 Shelby were originally to be Marchal units, but a recall replaced them with more reliable Lucas pieces. A few cars probably made it out the door with Marchals, but these lights would be more of a curiosity than a valuable rarity. *Nick Nicaise*

1969–70 GT350:	7.5
1969–70 GT500:	8
1969–70 GT350 convertible:	8
1969–70 GT500 convertible:	8.5

1969-1970 Shelby

1969 Shelby

In 1969 the trends of the past continued. Once again Ford Motor Co. upsized the Mustang, and by now it was getting lower, longer, wider, meaner, and, alas, heavier. Once again, the Shelby grew along with it.

Very few mechanical components were not right off the stock Mustang heavy-duty order sheet in 1969. The money that Ford spent—and it turned out to be a considerable sum—went almost entirely into the body. To many eyes, the result was the most attractive Shelby of all; it didn't have the high-performance modifications of the earlier cars—rather, it didn't have any high-performance mods that couldn't be bought on a stock Mustang—but it sure looked fantastic. There were, of course, some high-performance Mustangs by 1969 from which to pirate parts.

Unlike previous Shelbys, the 1969 model's

Pure-Shelby front end of 1969 GT350 can be expensive to replace or repair. The bumper, fiberglass panels, grille beading, hood clips, grille, and decal are all unique to the car; they're available at a price, but not from any Mustang graveyard. Check the entire cavity for cracks and other damage before signing up. *Nick Nicaise*

Twin hood stripes were a simple way for Shelby and Ford to differentiate 1970 Shelbys from the 1969 variety, which was of course an almost identical car. These are sometimes simply masked off while the rest of the car gets re-sprayed, so check for a telltale paint ridge along their edges. If found, the real perfectionist will have to have the entire hood repainted by someone who can really match colors well. *Nick Nicaise*

styling was taken seriously from the start, and the design was at last truly different from the Mustang it was based on. Only the roof, doors, and rear fenders were retained; forward of the A-pillar the car was unique down to its own front bumper. For the first time, considerable modeling and drawing went into the car's body. (Shelbys had become something of a running test bed for future Mustang styling, and Ford wanted to make sure it was done right.) There would be no more working from crash-test prototypes to develop the cosmetic package.

The reputable fiberglass supplier Owens-Corning, already cranking out body panels for the Corvette, supplied the panels that changed the look of the Shelby. The entire grille became a brightwork-surrounded cavity, with 7in headlights outboard and twin Lucas driving lights mounted under the bumper. The hood swept neatly all the way to the front lip of the grille and featured no less than five NACA ducts—two at the front to let cold air into the engine compartment, two at the back to remove it, and one in the center to feed air to the mandatory ram-air induction system on the engine. The airflow vents were treated to wire-mesh screens to prevent bugs, leaves, cats, and old beer cans from entering the engine bay.

The front fenders featured functional

Mustang and Shelby Growth Patterns, 1966, 1968, 1970

It's interesting to note that throughout Shelby Mustang production the wheelbase of the cars remained constant at 108in. Over the three bodystyle changes, the width increased from 68.2 to 70.9 to 71.8in; length went from 181.6 to 186.6 to 190.6in. Curb weight, of course, followed suit: Depending on equipment and counting big-blocks where available, the average 1966, 1968 and 1970 Shelby weighed about 2,950, 3,550, and 3,700lb, respectively.

scoops for brake cooling, as did the rears. On the convertibles, the rear brake scoops were in about the same location as they had always been. On the fastback, though—now called the SportsRoof—the duct was higher, up on the character crease. The tail again ended in a large fiberglass ducktail spoiler, and once more 1965 new-old-stock Thunderbird sequential taillights were fitted. A pair of sexy rectangular aluminum exhaust tips graced the center of the rear valance panel. Unfortunately, it was later realized that vapors from the vented gas cap directly over the exhaust tips could be ignited by a backfire. The vented caps were recalled and replaced with non-vented units, and tank ventilation was achieved through a hose exiting in the right-hand frame rail. After June 8, all cars were built with the vented system as standard equipment. Aftermarket vented caps should be replaced ASAP with the real thing.

All the unique body pieces, of course, make this an expensive car upon which to perform cosmetic restoration. Fortunately, the body panels used were of pretty decent quality and considerable girth; they're much stronger than one might expect, so cracking and delaminations are relatively uncommon.

Interiors were again Deluxe Mustang GT specification, primarily in black and white with red (vermillion) offered late in production. High-back bucket seats were standard on the Shelby while optional on other Mustangs; they were a worthwhile safety feature that prevented whiplash in rear-end collisions, so insist on them. Low buckets from other Mustangs are not only incorrect, they're needlessly dangerous. Wood-trim appliques were used throughout the interior, as were a plethora of Shelby and Cobra tags to remind the driver what he'd paid for. All these glued-on goodies can curl and fall off.

Placed directly in front of the passenger was a large clock, a bit out of the driver's line of sight but handy regardless. A unique console with driver-angled oil pressure and amp gauges was again used in the Shelby, along with the by-now traditional 8000rpm tach and 140mph speedometer. Inertial-reel shoulder harnesses protected SportsRoof driver and passenger, but the roll bar itself became more decorative than functional that

Despite the 1970 Shelby's heft, power-assisted disc brakes did an excellent job of hauling the car down from speed. There's nothing particularly troublesome about any Shelby's standard brakes (except the GT350H's MICO piggyback booster) so inspect and price them as you would the brakes of any other car. *Nick Nicaise*

year—it was thinner than before and now bolted to the sides, rather than the floor, of the car's interior. The attractive plastic cladding, of course, was retained on the convertible.

The Shelby's suspension system was identical to that of the Mustang Mach 1; the package consisted of stiffer springs and shocks, heavier front antiroll bar, and staggered rear shocks to control axle hop on the four-speed GT500 cars. The Mach 1 suspension handled quite well, and further modifications—still stiffer suspension, heavier antiroll bars and so on—are probably counterproductive; keep an eye out for excessive stress cracks on stiff-riding Shelbys.

The GT350's engine became the Ford 351, a completely reworked and enlarged version of the 302. Only the old 302 heads would interchange with those of the 351; everything else was different. (There was little point in swapping the heads even though it *was* possible; the 351s were more efficient than the 302s.)

With an aluminum intake manifold and 470cfm Autolite four-barrel carburetor, the GT350's Windsor engine did put out a respectable 290hp and 385lb-ft of torque. Cobra finned valve covers, made of aluminum, were of course added to the engine. There were certainly those who would rather have seen something like the high-revving Boss 302 engine in the GT350, but for the same output, Shelby Automotive figured it would go with the less-stressed, lower-revving, and considerably cheaper 351.

The killer 428 Cobra Jet engine again graced the GT500. (The KR designation was dropped before production began.) With something like two tons fully loaded to haul around, the Cobra Jet was the engine of choice for speed freaks. A cold-air induction hood, a $133 option on other Mustangs, was standard (technically designating the package 428 CJ-R, for ram air) on the Shelby. Quarter-mile times and speeds were noticeably—maybe a couple of tenths of a second and a few miles per hour—improved by the denser, cooler air the system fed to the

Anybody who derides the final Shelbys as detuned boulevard cruisers has never been on this side of one. GT500's 428 engine would shoot the car down a straight at warp speed. Many have been pretty badly abused because the gas pedal is just too tempting, and a lot of 428s show signs of internal wear because of it. A simple compression test often confirms the worst. *Nick Nicaise*

engine. Despite its size and high level of comfort, a GT500 with F70x15 tires would still cover the quarter mile in the tantalizingly low fourteens.

The GT350 could be fitted with a Ford FMX automatic transmission or a close-ratio four-speed gearbox as options; a wide-ratio four-speed Ford top-loader was standard equipment. Relatively few cars had this transmission. Most four-speed cars had the close ratio. The GT500 had a close-ratio box standard, a C-6 automatic as an option, and no wide-ratio manual transmission was available. A Traction-Lok limited-slip differential

could be ordered for a car that would see particularly heavy duty. Once more, the Traction-Lok is a bit noisy, so don't let it throw you.

There was only one wheel available on the Shelbys, a five-spoke aluminum and chrome steel 15x7in unit that was unique to the car. It was soon discovered that improper machining of the lug holes could lead to premature loosening of the wheel, so a recall was ordered and the lug holes were rechamfered on each wheel. Many cars received aftermarket wheels, of course, but this by and large ceased to be a dealer-installed change. For stock wheels, it's definitely worth adding some bucks to your offer; they're costly things to add later.

Shelby colors paralleled the regular production Mustang hues: three blues, two greens, two reds, an orange, one silver, one black, and a yellow. Taking a cue from Triumph, the long tape stripes—in blue, gold, black, or white—that ran down the beltline of the car carrying the GT350 or GT500 logo were made of reflective material for better visibility at night. A coiled snake graced the sail panels of Sports-Roof cars. (Any snake emblems on convertibles are most likely owner-installed.)

---

351 Engine Swaps

The 1969 GT350's engine would eventually be called the 351 Windsor, after its Windsor, Ontario, assembly plant. Although a fine performer in the low and middle rev ranges, the Windsor suffered from a limited head and porting design and never had the oomph to become a real hot-rod engine. That honor would go to the 351 Cleveland (for Cleveland, Ohio) that was introduced in 1970. Though the Cleveland and the Windsor started life on the same drawing board, by the time that distinction was made they were two different animals. The Cleveland's more efficient heads necessitated new coolant paths, so the two blocks and most of their components weren't interchangeable.

It was the more costly Cleveland that would see duty as Ford's high-performance small-block, most famously in the exotic De Tomaso Pantera. The Windsor, on the other hand, was less amenable to modification. You'll come across a number of 1969–1970 GT350s in which the owners have substituted a Cleveland for the Windsor; that swap was essentially the first logical step in hopping up the car. The two engines are readily identifiable by the fuel pump; the bolts are side to side on a Windsor and top and bottom on a Cleveland. Even though a Cleveland-equipped Shelby is likely to be faster than its unmodified brethren, of course, a car so equipped is unoriginal and less valuable than a stock example.

The decision to leave a hopped-up Shelby alone or bring it back to factory specification is up to you. With a 1969-1970 GT350, many owners opt for power over originality and just eat the difference in value.

Model nomenclature moved up to the beltline for 1969-70, and the decal became reflective. Tough to find, though, very tough to find. *Nick Nicaise*

All sorts of unique and costly bodywork resides at the car's tail as well as its nose. The aluminum exhaust collectors below the center of the bumper are close enough to the metal to lead to premature corrosion of the plating, so check this area well. *Nick Nicaise*

By 1969, Carroll Shelby's personal involvement with the Shelby automobiles had changed dramatically. Originally, of course, he was in charge of the whole ball of wax. As production of the Shelby Mustangs increased and Shelby's role in Ford's competition program decreased, Ford took a more and more active role in the affairs of the company. Shelby was pretty much forced into doing what he liked the least: fighting internal battles and power struggles within Ford, a company known almost as much for its politics as its automobiles.

Ford had helped to make the one-time Air Force pilot, one-time chicken rancher, and one-time racing driver into a rich man. But they had certainly not done that themselves; no one but Shelby could take credit for the tremendous success of the man in a number of different businesses. Carroll Shelby knew that as much as Ford would survive without him, he would do the same without Ford.

As Shelby Automotive degenerated more and more into a direct division of the Ford Motor Co., and Shelby himself attended more and more meetings and conferences, he began to realize that something was missing from the business: fun.

He also knew as well as Ford that the real reasons to have a Shelby Mustang at all were disappearing. The car was now competing with other Ford products as much as with those from other manufacturers, and Ford had fully achieved the performance image he had helped so much to build.

There was one other thing that Shelby realized, perhaps more keenly than everyone else: government regulations would soon make the sorts of cars Shelby liked to build a thing of the past. Even in 1969 it was obvious that federal emissions and safety guidelines would soon take a big toll on performance cars. When the crunch came, all that would be left, Shelby feared, were tape packages and mag wheels. Carroll Shelby did not like the idea of putting his name on big cars with weak engines; he did things the other way around.

Boss Mustangs:
Shelby Methods by Ford

Elsewhere in the Ford empire, two projects were going on without Shelby's assistance that looked for all the world like they had his fingerprints on them: the Boss 302 and Boss 429. Both homologation specials, these cars were very similar in concept and execution to what Shelby had done with the original Mustang back in 1964 and 1965.

The Boss 302, designed and sold as a streetable version of Ford's Trans-Am racing car, began life as a regular Mustang. But its engine was a Ford V-8 with suspiciously Shelby-like modifications: a strengthened block, four-bolt main-bearing caps, forged crank and connecting rods, aluminum high-rise intake manifold with a big Holley four-barrel carb, and heavily reworked heads with huge valves. With the artificial rev limiter removed, the Boss 302 would run to more than 7000rpm with ease.

The front shocks were braced, heavy-duty spindles were included, and the fenders were radiused to cover big tires below. Sound familiar?

The Boss 429, meanwhile, was built to satisfy NASCAR's 500 unit homologation rule, and its production paralleled early Shelby cars even closer. A separate line was set up at Kar Kraft in Brighton, Michigan, where the car's shock towers were moved outward to make room for a killer 429ci hemi-head Ford V-8. Then the Shelby-izing, sans Shelby, began. The car was outfitted with an oil cooler, fat antiroll bars and springs, even a trunk-mounted battery and 1in lower front suspension, old GT350 trademarks.

If Shelby had been able to retain control of his operations throughout the 1960s, one could theorize that both Boss Mustangs would actually have had Shelby written on them. As it was, though, Ford pulled in its operations and Shelby went further and further from the side of the business he really loved—building the fastest cars available. The Boss 302 and Boss 429 make excellent Shelby alternatives today for the collector; though prices have fluctuated wildly of late, it may pay to take a look if you don't care about getting the Shelby name.

Boss 429 (foreground) and 302 were Shelby-think products done by Ford on the Kar Kraft line. Both powerful and impressive (and virtually hand-made) cars, they're an alternative to Shelbys for many of the go-fast set. *Nick Nicaise*

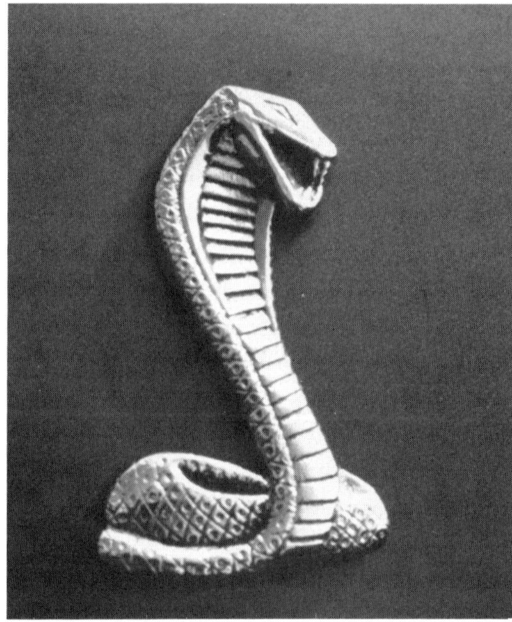

Engine badging at the top trailing edge of the front fender came right from the Ford parts bin, and coiled snake logo toward the rear is a common repro item. Unlike a lot of the 1969-70 trim, there's no problem finding these pieces. *Nick Nicaise*

Instead of charging up the works for the 1970 model, Shelby convinced Ford that it would be better to go out on top. The fantastic run that began with an order for 100 homologation specials would end after 1969, a year when buyer interest seemed to be leveling off along with Shelby's enthusiasm.

1970 Shelby

It's true that Shelby and Ford decided to call it quits after 1969, but things didn't quite work out that way. As the model year drew to a close, it was obvious that all of the 3,150 production cars and three prototype Shelbys built would not be sold by the end of the model year. In order to avoid having to unload the unsold cars at fire-sale prices, the decision came down to turn unsold 1969 Shelbys—a group of 789 cars that weren't necessarily the last ones built, just the last ones to be sent out to dealers—into 1970 models.

This was a relatively easy task mechanically, but a more difficult one legally. All Shelby Automotive did was add two hood stripes between the front and rear NACA vents. An evaporative control system to meet tougher emissions standards was required on all cars built after January 1, 1970, but no Shelbys were built after that date, and no cars built before January 1 (in effect, all 1969-70 Shelbys) were retrofitted.

A Boss 302 chin spoiler would round out the package, but that just meant throwing one in the trunk. The low spoilers had to be installed by the dealer or they'd get torn off while driving the car onto the carrier. That means, of course, that a lot of 1970 Shelbys have pretty banged-up spoilers these days. Replacements are available and fairly simple to mount.

Legally, however, there were a lot of government agencies that weren't exactly thrilled by the notion of reidentifying 1969 cars as 1970 models. This was neither illegal nor unethical, it just left a lot of room for shenanigans. It made the paper that went with the vehicles a confusing proposition—one that could lead to a lot of cars without registrations or registrations without cars.

All 1969 and 1970 Shelbys started out with 1969 VIN numbers stamped in four places: on a tag below the windshield, on another tag riveted to the driver's door, and on the inner housings of both front fenders. The 1969 VIN numbers all began with 9; 1970 numbers would have to replace them, as 1970 model VIN numbers started with a zero. The FBI (Federal Bureau of Investigation) was very nervous; so much so that it personally supervised the destruction of all the leftover 1969 ID plates.

Since state laws usually require only two visible ID tags, just the windshield and door

A unique center console graces the otherwise stock Mustang Deluxe interior package. (A smattering of coiled snakes were thrown in on top of the wooden appliques as well.) Warped or busted consoles are a major hassle to replace. *Nick Nicaise*

Shelby went to a thinner and less securely mounted roll bar for 1969, so these cars aren't as safe as earlier models. Still, some bar is better than none, which is what everybody else was offering. *Nick Nicaise*

plates were changed; the serial numbers in the fenders, which were invisible until the fenders were removed anyway, were left alone. Thus 1970 cars have the odd feature of VINs in which the year character (the first digit in the serial number) is a 9 for both 1969 and 1970 cars' "hidden" numbers. Don't let that throw you. That's the way they're supposed to be.

The cars that were updated to 1970 specifications were sold off with minimal fanfare, and Shelby's direct relationship with Ford came to a close.

One interesting sidelight from the 1970 model year was the Quarter Horse show car, seriously considered as a new top-of-the-line Mustang that would blend together the best of the Shelby and the regular production car. Essentially, this car had a Shelby front end grafted to a Boss 429 chassis and powerplant. It never saw production per se, but it definitely pointed toward Shelby's final hardware contribution to the Mustang program. In 1971, all Mustangs got a nose and fender treatment very similar to the one introduced on the 1969 Shelby. (Shelby's version, of course, looked better.)

And oh, maybe Shelby did contribute one other thing worth mentioning before he left Ford; in the terms of the Shelby-Ford divorce, Ford retained all rights to the Cobra name. The company ran it into the ground, sticking it onto almost everything, even the Pinto-based Mustang II—a motley little cur that ran the quarter mile about as fast as an asthmatic nun after a big church supper. Due to Ford's perhaps unfortunate skill at placing cars in films and television shows, that same Mustang II has given Cobra owners perhaps their most hated question: "A Cobra? Isn't that the little car that one of Charlie's Angels used to drive?"

Convertible 1969 GT500 is for some the ultimate Shelby. No longer the fastest cars on the road, they were among the most distinct; prices have risen accordingly. *Nick Nicaise*

Chapter 8

Shelby Dodges

Shelby Dodges	
Charger:	3
Charger (with Turbo I):	3.5
Charger GLH-S:	4.5
Omni GLH:	3
Omni GLH (with Turbo I):	3.5
Omni GLH-S:	5
Lancer (Turbo I):	2
Lancer (Turbo II):	3
CSX (Turbo I):	3
CSX (Turbo II)	3.5
CSX (Turbo IV):	5

As he had expected, the automobile industry changed dramatically in the years since Carroll Shelby and Ford Motor Co. parted ways. Cars were downsized, fuel economy and emissions became vitally important, and for a long, long time performance was a dirty word in Detroit. It was a shakedown that some lamented and others felt was overdue; whichever side you came down on, though, you agreed that everything indicated big-engine performance cars were gone for good.

At the same time that the auto market was changing, the executive slots at many of the car companies changed as well. John De-Lorean, Gene Bordinat, Ed Cole—a lot of the big names moved on, mostly into retirement.

Charger model's plastic nose piece is tough and durable, but the fit to the rest of the body isn't the greatest. Many people assume this means the car has been involved in a wreck, but it doesn't; that's just the way they came.

But after the biggest head hunt in the industry, the Chrysler Corporation wound up with a new man in charge: Lido "Lee" Iacocca, one of Shelby's most stalwart friends at Ford through the 1960s.

Iacocca was not, despite his acknowledged role in the original Mustang, a die-hard performance fan; he was a die-hard sales fan. A consummate blend of engineer and salesman, Iacocca saw the same big opportunity for sales in the early 1980s that he had seen in the early 1960s: Americans were ready for some real driving fun again. Who better to turn to than the old funster himself, Carroll Shelby?

These days, a number of the Dodge products bearing Shelby's name have become interesting enough to merit a club of their own. The Shelby American Automobile Club and Dodge-Shelby fans got together and decided to spin off a new owners group as a separate entity from the SAAC. The Shelby Dodge Automobile Club (c/o Mark Rhoades, 4011 Fleetwood Ave., Baltimore, Maryland 21206) performs the same sort of services and functions for Shelby Dodge owners that the SAAC delivers to its members.

Shelby Dodge Collectibility

In 1982, Carroll Shelby returned to the auto enthusiast's world by announcing that he was getting back into the business; he would be hot-rodding Dodges this time, not Fords, but it would be the same general idea. Of course the details would have to be different this time around. Instead of brute power from gas-swilling V-8 engines, Shelby would put a premium on handling and responsiveness over brute strength, and on real-world driving over racetrack prowess.

That's what the man said. As time went on Shelby Dodges got faster and faster, in many ways actually bettering the performance of the legendary GT350s and GT500s. But at this

Only a very sharp eye attached to a fast-reading brain can tell that this is no ordinary Omni. The discreetness of Shelby's decals always helped to downplay the fact that the GLH-S would run with some of the fastest sports cars in the world; it also slows the acquisition of tickets somewhat.

point in time they haven't come close to earning the reputation and romance—and therefore the collector value—of the Ford-Shelby products. There are three good reasons for this:

First, time. These cars haven't been around long enough to acquire collector interest; it takes at least ten years for most cars to become collectible.

A second reason is the cost of oil. Chrysler's assumption that V-8s were dead proved wrong when gas became cheap again, and enthusiasts won't show much interest in 175hp muscle cars while Detroit is still cranking out V-8s in the 220-300hp range.

A third factor accounting for Ford–Shelby products' value is racing history. Unlike the Shelby Fords, the Shelby Dodges' success in racing has been pretty much limited to less-publicized amateur series.

Cynics will add two more factors to the list: lack of initial enthusiasm, and the dilution of the breed. Chrysler-built, high-volume vehicles like the Shelby Turbo Z will only serve to lessen the collector impact of hot Shelby-built cars like the GLH-S and CSX models. In any case, one thing is relatively certain: unless fuel prices skyrocket again and renew interest in

Though rather uninspired in appearance, GLH-S wheels were honest cast aluminum and an impressive 15x6in in size. Light and robust, they should never be a problem.

high-efficiency performance, Dodge-Shelby vehicles will never attain the collectibility of Ford-Shelby models, even though in many

No matter how you approach it, the GLH-S just never looks much like a sports car, and its aerodynamics were pretty awful. Blacked-out, old-fashioned side mirror was standard on both sides of the car.

Most Shelby offerings used a tacked-on boost gauge to keep drivers apprised of turbo conditions. Self-regulated by a wastegate, the gauge was only really effective in letting driver know when to dump the clutch for a tire-chewing launch.

cases they're rarer cars. (And in many cases, darned *fast* cars.)

Beginning of the Line

Enthusiasts were at first a little timid about the whole notion of a Shelby-modified Dodge. For one thing, they realized that Chrysler simply didn't have that much hardware that looked like it could be hopped up. The company was surviving on economy platforms like the Dodge Charger and Plymouth Horizon TC3 (both K-car knockoffs known as the L-bodies), and its best corporate powerplant was a 2.2liter four-cylinder. The 2.2 was an OK passenger-car engine, but the thought of making it into something resembling a Shelby 289 or Cobra Jet 428 seemed, with some generosity, amusing at best. (Little did anyone realize that by 1992 the 2.2 would be netting 224bhp, very nearly the gross horsepower output of Shelby's 306 V-8s.)

The other fear among performance fans was that Shelby's projects would be a downright embarrassment, like the one already glimpsed from Alejandro De Tomaso, another of Iacocca's former Ford cronies. De Tomaso had put his name on a tarted-up version of the Horizon TC3, and the resulting "joint venture" was little more than a heinously ugly decalmobile. The thought that Carroll Shelby's name would be sullied in a similar way made Shelby American fans madder than a Ferrari owner with carb trouble.

They needn't have worried, though. Shelby turned his attention first to the L-body as De Tomaso had done, but this time the look was cool and restrained. A sophisticated two-tone cosmetic package of complementing silver and blue, matched CS-logo seats, restrained front and rear spoilers, cast alloy wheels, and blanked-out rear sail panels made the car look aggressive but not childish.

Attractive as they were, Shelby's modifications happily didn't end with the cosmetics. Shocks and springs were stiffened for improved response and stability, and the engine was pumped up to 107hp from the usual 94 through minor tuning tweaks. The handling was excellent (for those who liked front-wheel-drive cars, at least) and the acceleration was acceptable if not neck-snapping.

A five-speed transmission gave the Shelby Charger a good balance of economy and performance, but Chrysler's cable-operated shift was never the greatest. (Depending on adjustment, early Chrysler shifters can be notchy but workable, or a regular bag o' gears. Finding a mechanic who can do a good adjustment can be tricky and expensive, so look for reasonably clean shifts in any used Dodge-Shelby product.)

Enthusiasts approached the Shelby Charger tentatively at first—in fact, Dodge-Shelby sales would never be very large—but warmed to it quickly. If the car was not a GT350 for the eighties, nothing else was either. The Shelby Charger became, much to many people's surprise, a real alternative to the heavier Camaros and Mustangs that were teething their way into the 1980s. All in all, it was a fine car considering the restraints placed upon it.

One thing it wasn't, however, was especially cheap; in fact, most of the Dodge Shelbys weren't bargains despite the company's claims. Many models would outperform cars costing three and four times as much, but most buyers didn't compare performance as much as looks, reputation, and quality of assembly. To many, these cars weren't Porsches at a bargain, they were small Dodges at a higher price. The original Shelby Charger stickered out around $8,300, comparable to a 5.0liter HO (High Output) equipped Mustang GLX but well below the Mustang GT. It would outperform the Mustang, but it still *wasn't* a Mustang—it was a K-car.

As of 1991, early Shelby Chargers haven't bottomed out in value. From the standpoint of an investment, with their normally aspirated and relatively weak engines they will probably never be terrific buys. A fully optioned 1983 Camaro, made in much higher numbers, should still turn more of a profit over time.

So far the Shelby Dodges are proving to be pretty tough in their major components. Structural rust doesn't seem to be a big problem, and the metal, plastic, and cloth hold up about as well as in any other early-eighties automobile. With the exception of strut bushings, which seem to be overtaxed by the Shelby-specification Koni shocks, the weak spots for Shelby-Dodge cars are the same as for any other Chrysler L- or K-body. Quality of assembly is a little dodgey (forgive the pun), so rattles and buzzing sounds may abound; a few circuits with screwdrivers and wrenches usually get things solid again. Head gaskets are a notorious problem with the 2.2liter motor, so check for weeping at the head-block junction, water in the oil, and bubbles or foam in the coolant while the engine is running. Alternators are a major weak link, and look for paint that is chipping or peeling on the bumper-air dam assemblies.

Approximately 200 Shelby Chargers from the 1984 model year came with automatic transmissions, making them reasonably rare. Whether these cars will ever achieve enough collector status to make this a valuable option is open to question, but for some collectors it is a convenience they'll like. Another relative rarity is the 300 odd 1986 cars with reversed blue-on-silver paint schemes.

Omni GLH

The next car to come under Carroll Shelby's eye was the Dodge Omni, a Volkswagen

Twin Bosch driving lights on GLH-S harkened back to the early days of the Shelby Mustang. Not just for show, they really did illuminate the road in use—of course that meant getting out and removing the standard plastic covers, which most people never bothered to do.

Sleek fastback lines of the Charger GLH-S were perhaps a little more appropriate to the car's potential speed than the Omni GLH-S shell. The Charger body weighed more, though, and its drag figures were barely an improvement over the more plebian model's—it is in fact a slight tick slower than the boxier four-door through the quarter mile.

Shelby windshield decal was an absolute staple of the line. Some have been removed by owners who didn't like the looks, but replacements are usually still available through Dodge dealers.

Comfortable and attractive CS-logo seats were among the very first additions Shelby added when he came aboard at Dodge. The cloth center sections stain easily, however, and the silver vinyl outer panels are often scuffed. The vinyl can be easily re-dyed, but replacing the cloth may be difficult when the time comes.

Rabbit-like four-door living in relative obscurity. For the Shelby GLH (reputedly for Goes Like Hell), the Pentastar boys took a basic Omni shell, dropped in a 110hp engine, substantially tightened up the underpinnings, and added restrained identifying graphics and cast wheels. The result was a Q-ship that followed the thinking of VW's successful Rabbit GTI—a sports car that looked like a people hauler.

In truth, the GLH was more Austin Mini Cooper than Volkswagen GTI: a raucous, rattling, buzzing, maybe even ugly little shoebox that was a ball to drive and a respectable performer by the numbers. While the VW was a firm, unbending, rewarding miniature of stolid German performance, the GLH was tongue-in-cheek; its exterior and interior equipment shouted "cheap" and its compliance over the road was harsh. At the same time, though, the driver wore a big smile and laid down rubber from two squirrely front tires. No cop would ever suspect a GLH driver of breaking the law, while no autocrosser expected anything less. The GLH was as quick as or quicker than the Charger, and at a price of more than $1,200 fewer dollars it constituted a real bargain.

In 1985, things got more serious with the introduction of the GLH Turbo. Chrysler, recognizing early on the apparent limitations of a company strategy built around a 2.2liter four, had done extensive testing with forced induction systems to raise the output of the engine. What they came up with by 1985 was a turbocharged, 146hp mill with 9psi of boost and an impressive reliability record. The turbo was water cooled to prevent coking (the accumulation of burnt oil residue), the main killer of turbo systems. With the turbo option the GLH became one of the quickest cars in America, a real wolf in sheep's clothing.

Under the skin, the GLH was of course the same car as the Shelby Charger, so watch for the same maladies. All Omni-bodied cars seem more prone to minor damage, though, probably because people in parking lots don't show them the respect they would show a racier, more expensive looking automobile. The front spoiler of the GLH is often damaged, but replacements are available, and flaking on the blackout trim can be a problem on early cars.

One other thing to watch out for with all turbocharged GLHs (and the later turbocharged Chargers) is fuel pump cavitation; when the system fails, a tremendous buzzing sound goes through the car "like a hive of bees," according to one Shelby expert. Dodge dealers quickly received a service bulletin on the problem, so later cars weren't affected and the repair for earlier cars is well understood.

The Skunk Works

By 1986, the Shelby-Dodge collaboration had gone from pure driving fun to serious performance fun. Shelby set up his own manufacturing operation in Whittier, California, the Dodge Shelby Performance Center. Colloquially known as the Skunk Works (in honor of the Lockheed division where Kelly Johnson created the SR-71, U-2, Starfighter, and other record-breaking aircraft), Shelby's charter was to modify Dodge products beyond the ability of a Chrysler assembly line. It seemed to be Venice and Los Angeles International Airport all over again.

In truth, the Skunk Works was quite a bit more sophisticated than Shelby's earlier haunts. Its computerized dynos and a permanent skidpad-slalom course reflected the changes in the way cars were built in the 1980s. Performance tests would no longer include a subjective run along the factory's back fence. Now Shelby looked at *objective*, computer-timed runs on his own small proving grounds.

The first car to be modified at Whittier was the GLH Turbo; Shelby purchased production cars from Chrysler with the 146hp engine and modified them on his own small line as he had done with the original GT350. The first thing attended to was the engine. A larger turbocharger was added, along with an intercooler (to cool, and therefore make

Tinted moon roof adds much-appreciated airiness to the relatively confined cockpit of the Shelby Charger. Because the basic Charger layout was so Spartan, all of Shelby's upholstery, trim, and accessory additions made a tremendous difference to driver enjoyment.

denser, the incoming air), a revised intake manifold and tuned runners, and the necessary attendant electronic control modifications. Also included were multipoint fuel injection, larger fuel rails, a bigger radiator, and a maximum-boost bump from 9psi to 12psi.

The result was called Turbo II, a 175bhp, 175lb-ft of torque engine. Because of the more careful assembly Shelby gave his cars, this powerplant was even stouter than the surprisingly robust stock unit, and head gasket worries are noticeably reduced.

One thing to watch out for, though, is the Turbo II's oil diet. Shelby recommended using Mobil 1 synthetic oil in all Turbo II engines to protect the turbo and internal bearings. Many owners fell off this regimen due to the synthetic lubricant's higher initial cost. For some reason, a car that's been fed a steady diet of Mobil 1 or even regular high-quality motor oil seems to run fine, but a car that's been switched from one to the other repeatedly often develops bearing and seal troubles. You should ask the owner, without mentioning specific brands, what sort of oil he or she has been using in the car.

Once the underpinnings were suitably firmed up, Shelby attached the GLH-S (for Goes Like Hell–Squared) moniker and produced 500 examples for 1986. While the original GLH and GLH Turbo had been a bit harsh and rattly, the added power of the GLH-S made for a car that was a downright buzz box. As much as Shelby put into the engine bay and suspension, the cars were still mostly assembled by Chrysler and some things were never bolted together all that well. Don't let a few rattles and panel gaps scare you away from this car—they're perfectly normal, if you want to see it that way. (In fact, these things are reminiscent of the way GT350s were originally delivered.) Because of its rarity, history, performance, reliability and sneaky econobox looks, the GLH-S could be a legitimate collectible in the long run.

In a well-publicized showdown, *Hot Rod* magazine organized a challenge between a 1965 GT350 and a preproduction GLH-S at Willow Springs International Raceway in Rosamond, California, one of the GT350's home tracks. It was the classic clash between old and new: 306 gross hp in a heavier, less rigid rear-wheel-drive platform versus 175 net hp in a stiffer, smaller front-wheel-drive car. To the surprise of adherents of both schools, the match was essentially a draw—the power advantage of the Ford was negated by the lighter weight and twenty years of advanced tire and suspension technology. The Dodge, in fact, surprised a few people by even nosing out the Ford in quarter-mile acceleration. It

Shelby dropped the long-running two-tone paint scheme when the Skunk Works-built Charger

GLH-S arrived (left). Dodge-built Charger Turbos stuck with it at the same time.

might have been heresy to the classic Shelby camp, but it was music to Lee Iacocca's ears.

1987: Shelby Lancer, Charger and CSX

The Skunk Works took on three more projects after the 1986 GLH-S run drew to a close. One would be the Lancer, a sporty-looking but dowdy four-door sedan also sold by Chrysler as the LeBaron GTS. The notion came from Shelby's desire to build cars with broader appeal than the boy-racer GLH-S; hence the eurostyle modifications to a certified people hauler. Four hundred Shelby Lancers got the Turbo II treatment along with the expected chassis and wheel modifications, while another 400 got a Turbo I engine and leather interior, Pioneer compact disc player, and automatic transmission. As before, Shelby was testing the waters of more touring-oriented performance. With a leather-wrapped steering wheel, one-piece aluminum wheels with Goodyear Gatorbacks, tinted power windows, power locks, and a high-zoot sound system, the Lancer was definitely shooting for the luxury end of the performance spectrum.

The Lancer (along with all 1987 and later Shelbys but the Dakota pickup) received rear disc brakes at the Whittier plant. New to Shelby Automotive was a set of Formula GP shocks and struts from Monroe and antiroll bars a full one and one-sixteenth inch and one and one-eighth inch in diameter front and rear, respectively.

At the same time the Lancer was being modified, Shelby realized there was no reason why the GLH-S powertrain couldn't be adapted to the sporty Charger bodyshell. It was, and an instant Charger GLH-S was created. Identified mostly by its color (black with silver accents), functional hood grate, and "Intercooled" script on the power bulge, these cars combined the speed of the GLH-S with a more appropriate shape. By then, of course, the novelty of the Turbo II engine package had worn off a bit and the car received less attention than it was due—a real problem for collectors down the road, as initial enthusiasm is one of the most important factors in later values. Charger GLH-S production ran double that of the Omni GLH-S, to 1,000 cars rather than 500, which won't help, and the Omni's larger interior makes it more convenient as an everyday driver.

The Charger GLH-S was also, due to weight and distribution differences, just a tick slower than the Omni GLH-S; both cars covered the quarter mile in a reported (but maybe optimistic) 14.7 seconds at 94mph, but the Omni was quicker off the line by a hair and registered 0.88 on the skidpad to the Charger's 0.84. Admittedly, these are differences that only the nerdiest of engineers would quibble over, but they do contribute more to the status of the Omni GLH-S over its sleeker-looking brother.

The third Shelby offering was based on the Dodge Shadow, an appealingly styled small two-door. Known as the Shelby CSX, this car received the Turbo II with all the concomitant goodies; 750 units came out of Whittier in 1987. Because of its small size and the more

Subtle trunk spoiler helped to differentiate the early Shadow-based CSX models from their econobox kin. Although small changes like this were never enough to attract large groups of buyers to the Skunk Works cars, production numbers were always kept small enough that it didn't matter; hence their rarity today.

photogenic Charger and Lancer being offered simultaneously, the CSX probably didn't receive all the notice it was due. The 175hp in the small Shadow body made for exciting performance to say the least; it ran 0-60mph in a hair over 7 seconds, quarter miles in a tick over 15. Monroe Formula GP struts and shocks suspended the car on its aluminum wheel-Goodyear Gatorback combination.

The CSX continued as a Shelby project for the next two years in interesting forms. In 1988, Shelby reprised his Hertz Rent-a-Racer gig by building 1,500 CSX-Ts for the Thrifty car rental outfit. These cars used a standard Turbo I engine from Chrysler with no modifications, and can be best identified by their CSX-T graphics on the lower rocker panels. Most were white with silver bottoms, but a small number—something shy of 200—were black.

Thrifty advertised the car heavily, and at $35 a day they weren't a bad deal. Each received a signed and numbered plaque on the dash, and they were sold off at bargain-basement prices once they outlived their usefulness to Thrifty. Despite what common sense might tell you, rental agencies usually keep their cars in good shape; don't be scared away from a CSX-T just because a lot of different people have driven it.

The CSX's grand finale, however, would come after Thrifty left the scene.

1989: Turbo IV CSX and Dakota

This would be the last year of Shelby's contract with Dodge as a constructor, and apparently the last year of the Dodge-Shelby automobile from Whittier.

The CSX again returned, this time as the carrier of Shelby's new Turbo IV powerplant,

Intercooled Turbo II engine made almost as much real power as some of Shelby's later Ford V-8s, yet needed just 2.2liters of displacement. Turbo II engines have proven extremely robust so long as synthetic oil has been used as specified. Dodge-built ancillaries like A/C compressor and alternator have not been so lucky, so listen for clunks and rattles with a mechanic's stethoscope.

The Shelby Dodge Auto Club actively supports autocross programs to get owners involved with their cars. What they've learned through competition about suspension setups and the car's strong and weak points will be invaluable to any owner or buyer—it's a resource well worth tapping.

Lancers—both those from Dodge and Shelby—combined performance, luxury, and bang for the buck, but never really captured people's imagina-tions. Though a great used-car performance buy, they probably won't appreciate much. *Dodge, Courtesy Michael Lamm*

one of the most sophisticated engines of its day. Still based on the old 2.2liter block, this time the car received a unique variable-nozzle Garrett turbo which eliminated the need for a waste gate. A series of vanes directed airflow to the turbine impeller, which resulted in more direct control of turbo speeds and therefore engine output. Turbo lag—which was never *terribly* bad to begin with—was reduced even further, and while horsepower figures stayed pat at 175, torque jumped significantly to roughly 205lb-ft. The 1989 Shelby CSX, which had trouble getting attention against the Firebirds, Mustangs, Thunderbirds, and Corvettes written up in the enthusiast press, was one of America's fastest cars, hitting 60mph in less than 7 seconds.

Shelby pulled out all the stops for this one: a five-speed Getrag gearset, 15in Fiberide (lightweight reinforced fiberglass) wheels, and Monroe Formula GP shocks in addition to the usual stiffer-is-better suspension system. The graphics were tasteful to the point of near nonexistence, reduced to CSX logos around the car and an outlined "Shelby"

script at the top of the windshield. Spoilers and side skirts were integrated nicely to the body shape, making for an understated package overall.

Inside, things were a little less restrained. In addition to the now-usual Shelby-autographed leather steering wheel, a repeating "Shelby" pattern was woven into the seat and door panel material in mildly contrasting colors.

Though still too new to be anywhere near bottoming out in value, someday the Turbo IV engine and all the attendant high-tech hardware may qualify this car as a collectible. The newness of the variable-nozzle turbo and plastic wheels, of course, may also come back to haunt it; so far, there's no consensus on the system's long-term reliability.

Shelby's other 1989 project was an old-fashioned engine swap for 1,500 Dakota pickups. The suspension and underpinnings were left alone as they already featured rear-wheel ABS, a front antisway bar, and Monroe gas shocks from the Dodge parts bin. The conversion consisted of Shelby graphics, a streamlined light bar (that's lawyer talk for a roll bar that may or may not do a whit of good in an accident), a front air dam and fender extensions, some interior dressing (including embroidered "Shelby" inserts on the bench seat and door panels), unique five-spoke aluminum wheels, and the substitution of a 318ci V-8 engine for the Dakota's usual six. The 318, which survived in Chrysler's truck operations from the olden days, got a dual throttle-body injection intake system good for 175hp and 270lb-ft of torque.

Though a big hit where truck fanciers congregate, whether that market will respond with anything like a buying spree ten or twenty years down the road is doubtful. Classic trucks have never had anything remotely like the appreciation rate of cars, so don't pin your kids' college education fund on this one.

Shelby by Dodge

While Carroll Shelby was constructing cars out in Whittier, California, Chrysler built Dodges to Shelby's way of thinking on their own production lines. These cars are generally not as well assembled as the ones from Whittier (which boast stronger engines) and they're generally more common. Whether they will ever be true collectibles is doubtful, since they lack the cachet of being either the first of the line or hand-assembled Whittier vehicles. Still, the entry-level enthusiast will find a lot of fun to be had behind their wheels.

Later Chrysler-made vehicles like the Shelby Daytona Turbo Z and rare 1989 Shelby-badged but Dodge-built Lancer are often fine cars, but there's really not enough of a Shelby tie-in to make them potential collectibles. On Dodge's former glory car, the Daytona, Shelby's name was applied rather the same way Chevrolet put IROC logos on Camaros, and it meant about as much. Of course when Dodge took over the IROC series for themselves, guess what moniker replaced Shelby's on the Daytona. . . .

Dodge-built Daytona Shelby had all the right stuff, but lacked the Shelby-built cachet that would make them particularly good investments. Like many Mopars, their appreciation rate will probably trail a Firebird or Mustang of similar vintage. *Dodge, Courtesy Michael Lamm*

Chapter 9

GT40

GT40:	10
GT40 Mk. II:	10.5
GT40 Mk. III:	10
GT40 Mk. IV:	11
Lightweights, Mirages, Prototypes, etc.:	11

The GT40 can be traced directly to a merger deal that Ford and Ferrari discussed in the early 1960s. Henry Ford II and Lee Iacocca were enamored with Italian sports cars, and buying out Ferrari seemed like a good way to rub some Latin lustre off on Ford's regular products. But while Ferrari was receptive at first, the negotiations eventually turned ugly and a major rift resulted. Jilted and angry, Ford's development of a Le Mans-winning racer became almost a *fait accompli*; Hank the Deuce was not a man to be snubbed, and the car that would go on to win four straight runnings of Le Mans would be his weapon of revenge.

After negotiations with Ferrari collapsed,

Some racing GT40s were modified to receive the "Gurney bump," a teardrop-shaped dome over the driver's seat to accommodate Dan Gurney's head height. A number of other cars, however, have received this simply as a neat addition put in by private owners. *Nick Nicaise*

The biggest gathering of GT40s to ever take place occurred at Watkins Glen more than two decades after Ford racing program ended. Almost a third of the entire production run is represented in this photo, and an example of the early prototype roadsters graces the right of the front row. *Nick Nicaise*

Leo Beebe was tapped to head a new department from Dearborn, Ford Advanced Vehicles (F.A.V.), founded and funded with one goal in mind—to whip all comers, but *especially* Enzo Ferrari, at racing's highest level.

F.A.V. went shopping for a starting point on which to build, and after John Cooper pointed them toward Eric Broadley's door at Lola, they came across perhaps the most advanced sports car in the world at the time. Broadley's Lola GT was a monocoque-chassised, aerodynamic, mid-engined, Ford-powered, absolutely tiny racer that suffered only from lack of development funds. Ford officials would soon fix that—or so they thought.

They began developing a new chassis in England while engineers in the United States ironed out the body and aerodynamics. The main players would be F.A.V. (on both sides of the Atlantic) and Holman & Moody, the American stock car outfit. At first, Shelby was only tapped for two lesser jobs on the periphery: to handle stateside racing (and street sales) when the time came, and to use his experience and charm to shepherd the car through Europe's byzantine racing politics.

The new car, named GT40 because it sat 40in high (well, 40.5 really), made its first appearance at Le Mans in 1964. In finished form, the GT40 used a steel semi-monocoque (it was reinforced with square tubes) chassis, double-wishbone front and transverse link/lower wishbone rear suspensions, vented disc brakes, Borrani wire wheels, a single four-barrel carb on a production 260 with all the traditional Shelby trimmings, a Colotti four-speed transmission, and two huge fuel cells, one in each outboard rail. (Both of the Italian additions would soon be scrapped, the Borranis for their narrowness and the Colotti because of its extreme unreliability. The trucky, non-synchro ZF five-speed soon became standard.)

Of the three prototypes entered at Ford's first Le Mans, two had previously been run for less than four hours total. All of them DNF'd, and by the end of the year the GT40s had a perfect record—ten starts, ten retirements. They showed tremendous promise but simply wouldn't hold together. Ford's initial confidence began turning into embarrassment.

For 1965 they turned directly to Shelby for assistance. As long as the Cobras were winning races and keeping the blue oval in the limelight, the GT40 debacle was not as embarrassing as it could have been; but it was nevertheless sucking up a huge chunk of funds, and unless some positive results could be gained soon the entire racing program looked fit to fall apart.

Shelby applied his standard break-it-and-fix-it testing methods to the cars along with a good dose of common sense, while Ford itself made considerable strides with its computers. Two of the earliest changes, even predating Shelby's direct involvement, had been the fitting of a full-race Cobra 289 in place of the earlier 260 and a number of body updates to tame the car's high-speed handling. On February 28, 1965, a pair of Viking Blue and white GT40s took first and third at Daytona, bracketed by two Daytona Coupes. A second-place finish at Sebring one month later indicated that the cars were ready for Le Mans.

Six GT40s were entered, two of them 427-equipped monsters known as the GT40 Mk. II. But a win there was still not to be, and it would be another full year before Ford finally captured the 24-hour race that was its ultimate goal. Frustrated and embarrassed, Shelby and Ford undertook one of the most exhaustive race-car development programs of all time, even going so far as to hook the severed rear end of a GT40 to a computer-controlled dyno and running two simulated Le Mans races back to back.

In 1966, no less than thirteen entries—eight computer-honed, battle-proven Mk. IIs and five privately entered small-block cars—took off at the start. One day later the first, second, and third-place positions were all held by GT40 Mk. IIs, which cruised across the finish line three abreast. By 1967 a com-

With the nose piece off for easy servicing, the GT40's basically simple nature is apparent. Everything is pretty well exposed and even the bracing for the radiator could be swapped out without much fuss. *Nick Nicaise*

pletely new car, the GT40 Mk. IV, was racing at Le Mans, and it, too, won handily.

For 1968, the FIA put a displacement cap of 3.0liters on prototypes and 5.0liters on sports cars, effectively killing off the all-conquering 7.0liter Mk. II and Mk. IV Fords. Ford officials felt that they had accomplished what they set out to do, and happily withdrew from international sports car competition. Undaunted, however, John Wyer continued campaigning lightened small-block derivatives, known as Mirages, and took Le Mans again in 1968 and 1969, albeit not nearly so easily as before. Even after Ford's withdrawal, it was not until Porsche's all-conquering 917s arrived in 1970—again campaigned by Wyer—that the GT40's reign was truly over.

The Cars

One of the most fascinating things about the GT40 is that it was never exclusively a racing car. After an even dozen prototypes were built and campaigned—five small-block coupes, five small-block roadsters, and a pair of Mk. IIs—Ford built a first run of fifty "production" GT40Ps to meet sports car class rules. But all of these cars were *not* intended for the track—street versions were built as well, some receiving carpeted sills and floors, softer springs, a two-plate (in place of the normal three-plate) clutch, and (on the road-only Mk. III models, of which seven were built) a unique four-headlamp nose and the reversion to Colotti four-speed transaxles. Ford even printed up sales brochures for the road-going cars, and their success was such that production continued in fits and spurts after the original fifty were snapped up.

There's tremendous variety among the GT40 fold, of course, and I won't trouble you with all the ins and outs here. Entire books, and good ones, are available to anyone in-

Even a smallish 289 became something of a squeeze when asked to fit between the GT40's rear bulkhead and ZF transaxle. Complicating matters was the Indy-style "bundle of snakes" exhaust system, which actually added a noticeable amount of horsepower over the standard Cobra system. *Nick Nicaise*

Small-block-powered Mirages under Gulf sponsorship carried the GT40 on for two years after Ford withdrew from racing. The FIA saw them as modified versions of the production model and allowed them to remain classified as sports cars. John Wyer built just three of them, which makes them among the rarest of all examples. *Nick Nicaise*

clined to sort them all out. Suffice it to say, though, that, in general, the later in the production run a GT40 came along, the more interesting it is.

After sweeping Le Mans convincingly in 1966, Ford returned the next year with the GT40 Mk. IV, a radical aluminum-honeycomb, full-monocoque racer with one of the most gorgeous bodies ever to hit a track. The dozen aluminum chassis on which the Mk. IVs would ride were called J-chassis, and only four were originally built into Mk. IVs. One of these was destroyed, and the last, originally unbodied, J-chassis was much later privately converted to Mk. IV specs. The remainders were either never bodied, built as open Can Am cars, or used as aerodynamic test beds for the later "production" racers.

Also of note were the three Mirage cars built by John Wyer after Ford pulled out of FIA competition, and the five lightweight— two small-blocks and three big-blocks—

GT40s constructed by Alan Mann of England. Even rarer than the rest, all these cars sit at or near the top of the GT40 price chart.

By and large, however, most GT40s came as steel-chassis, small-block-powered street and racing cars, and both types frequently swapped roles as they were converted from one use to the other during their lives. The difference between them was that slight. A GT40's current configuration no doubt reflects a fascinating history of its own, but it's not necessarily indicative of the car's original specifications.

Some liberties have been taken with GT40s over the years; there are a lot more cars out there with "Gurney bumps" in their roofs than Dan Gurney himself ever drove. These sorts of changes don't seem to pull too much off the car's price, however, though a historically accurate model with a solid racing history is always going to be more valuable than a modified also-ran.

And speaking of value and these cars—well, people do. GT40s never came cheap, and even when they were little more than obsolete street and racing cars in the early 1970s, their prices never dropped below about $40,000. Today the sky's the limit, but the relatively high production numbers (134, give or take a car or two) have kept them from the insane realm of Ferrari GTOs and the like. Suffice it to say that any legitimate GT40 is worth, and will remain worth, the equivalent of a *particularly* nice house, the kind that comes with two pools and servants' quarters. Models with extreme rarities like original air conditioning and left-hand drive can add a six-digit figure to the bill.

There are a number of GT40 replicas on the road today and, like most replicas, some are better and some are worse. None, of course, will be much of an investment compared to a similarly-priced thoroughbred, but at about the same FOB price as an Acura NS-X, they make interesting drivers. With the help of original players like John Wyer and Len Bailey, Safir Engineering of England built the first and, arguably, best of the true replicas. Safir and Wyer constructed a bit more than a dozen well-respected cars (called Mk. Vs) using a fair number of original parts and jigs. While the 1980s moved on other players entered the field, including the recent arrival of ERA with an admittedly impressive offering. One is tempted to offer the standard warnings about forgeries being passed off as the real thing, but the original GT40 histories are generally quite well known, as the SAAC has

Borrani wire wheels that were fit to the earliest cars look great, but they were soon superceded by solid wheels which were stronger and wider. *Nick Nicaise*

taken on the task of following these cars. As always, if something sounds too good to be true it probably is, and with this much dough on the line only a fool would leap without doing some very serious looking beforehand.

Being race cars, most GT40s are relatively simple to reconstruct and repair. (The aluminum J-chassis cars are perhaps an exception, although this type of material is not nearly the mystery today that it was in 1967.) And being steel, they are as likely to fall foul of time as the next machine; rust seems endemic *everywhere* beneath the GT40's fiberglass skin, and a real expert should check out any car that's up for sale. Because the car's very registration plate is so valuable, however, even a seeming write-off can be brought back for a fraction of its finished value. The GT40s are big-league collector cars with big-league prices, and most of us can only hope to cadge an occasional ride in the passenger's seat, which, if you ever get the opportunity, can be the thrill of a lifetime.

Mk. IV GT40 brought a full aluminum monocoque to the GT40 program. Just three survived their racing days and a fourth has been created from an unbodied J-chassis tub. *Nick Nicaise*

Shelby Trans-Am Cars

1966

For 1966, the SCCA announced what would become one of the most hotly contested racing classes of the decade: the Trans-American Sedan Championship. Aimed at cars with four seats instead of two, it dovetailed perfectly with the pony and muscle cars suddenly hitting the American road. The interesting series of cars campaigned by Shelby's forces in Trans-Am deserve some mention.

Trans-Am was the most glamorous of a whole new group of Sedan series laid out like earlier sports car classes: A-Sedan for cars of 2.0 to 5.0liters; B-Sedan for 1.3 to 2.0liters; C-Sedan for 1.0 to 1.3liters; and D-Sedan for cars under 1.0liter in displacement.

At first the cars were kept virtually stock externally, with enough leeway allowed on the inside to make them into racers. The GT350 was ready-made for this kind of racing, but there was a hitch—Shelby had already classified it as a two-seater for B-Production sports car racing, and he couldn't have it both ways. So Shelby and Ford decided to produce a limited number of cars that were internally GT350s but outwardly production Mustangs, starting with a stock 289 notchback and performing most of the GT350 R-model modifications gave them essentially an instant race car.

The only real differences between the R-model and the Trans-Am car—aside from the notchback body and graphics, of course—were the things that the Sports Car Club of America wouldn't allow Shelby to do. Stock wheels had to be used without the R-model's aggressive flares (although American "R Model" magnesium wheels were allowed), no non-stock body additions like the front valance or hood scoop were allowed (but both bumpers could be removed), the interiors had to have full upholstery and headliners, and all the window glass and frames had to be stock and functional. (So much for the nifty aerodynamic back glass and the no-crank plexiglass side windows.) The SCCA later relented somewhat and let Shelby's Trans-Am cars race with wider wheels and rolled rear fender edges. Another modification allowed was a small rectangular notch in the stock steel Mustang front valance; this, like the notch on the R-models' valances, funneled air to an oil cooler.

Shelby ordered two batches of ten slightly special white notchbacks from San Jose, enough to campaign a factory effort and sell turn-key customer cars as well. Along with the development prototype (which was purchased from a local dealer), these cars went into the Shelby pipeline and came out as seventeen Group 2 (named for the FIA Appendix J, Group 2 regulations the SCCA deemed they must meet) Trans-Am racers and four Group 1 rally cars. All came as white 289 notchbacks with four-speed transmissions, a 9in rear end with Detroit Lockers, export shocks and brace, front discs, foglamps (from the Mustang GT package), and heavy-duty front springs.

Override traction bars were added along with all the other R-model suspension mods, a good clue to a car's Shelby heritage as few other race shops bothered to install them. The presence of these bars doesn't make a car a Shelby racer, but the lack of them would be a good indication against that claim. (Many other Trans-Am Mustangs built from scratch used aftermarket Shelby parts extensively, so the picture does indeed get cloudy. A no-name Trans-Am car can be an excellent—and potentially inexpensive—vintage racer, but of course it won't be worth as much as a Shelby-built car.)

Considering the roll that Shelby and Ford were on, it's not surprising that the 1966 Trans-Am program resulted in a manufacturer's title. Thank heavens, too; the big competition that year was the Plymouth Barracuda, and that would have left an awfully sour taste in the mouths of Ford fans. Of the twenty-one Group 2 and Group 1 cars produced in 1966, almost a third are presently unaccounted for. Start looking in barns and junkyards, folks. If you find a car that appears to be legit, contact the SAAC with the serial number for verification because they have them all on file.

1967

Something of a transition year for Trans-Am, 1967 was a halfway point between a gentleman's race series and a big-dollar, high-stakes manufacturer slugfest. The stock-looking cars brought big crowds, and manufacturers knew how important it was to win when their front-line offerings were being paraded around the track. Ford and GM struck at the Trans-Am bait and got seriously hooked, while Chrysler saw where it was all going—toward ever-bigger bucks for an ever-smaller chance of victory—and put on the brakes. (Chrysler did return in 1970, however.)

Ford contracted Shelby to run a two-car team for 1967, but to downplay the factory's involvement one car ran under Gulf and the other under Terlingua Racing Team markings. Ford also fielded two Cougars with Bud Moore, who tapped Dan Gurney and Parnelli Jones as drivers. Chevrolet, meanwhile, looked to Roger Penske to campaign the new Camaro with Mark Donohue behind the wheel.

Shelby again built additional customer cars, running up a total of twenty-six; one prototype and four racers stayed at Shelby American, and the rest went to privateers.

The 1967 Trans-Am cars relied heavily once more on the information and research that had been done for the GT350 R-model. Suspensions again mirrored the original solutions of lowered upper front A-arms, override traction bars and so on. Very minor tuning differences could compensate for the slightly bigger Mustang platform of 1967, and the rest of the components were by then a proven, debugged package. As for the bodies, again there were no fiberglass add-ons allowed and the interiors, glass, headliners, seats and other components were still in the cars. Insulation and carpeting were gone, but the rules were very specific about what could and couldn't be eliminated. Wider wheels and slightly flared fenders were allowed, and again Shelby opted for five-spoke American Racing units. A quick-fill cap to a 32gal fuel tank poked right out of the trunk lid.

The cars' engines, however, were substantially reworked. Big valves and a hot cam graced the 289, which was topped by a pair of 600cfm Holley four-barrels on an aluminum intake manifold. Sewer pipe-sized tubular exhaust headers completed the heavy-breathing layout, and as usual the engines were balanced, blueprinted, and dyno-tuned before installation.

As 1967 progressed, the Shelby and Moore cars remained impressive while the Chryslers fell further and further off the pace. But as the twelve-race calendar wound down, an ominous force started making its presence felt: the blue and yellow Camaros of Penske and Donohue. Chevrolet's chosen team would become a steamroller, but for 1967 it was too little, too late.

With one point between teams at the last race of the year, cars dropped out until it became Ronnie Bucknum's Mustang versus Dan Gurney's Cougar for the title. By then, circumstances had given Bucknum a healthy lead over Gurney's Cougar, but there was more racing to be done and Bucknum's temperature needle started to creep up. And up.

And up. Gurney drove as if chased by Beelzebub, but he couldn't do it. Bucknum won the race and the title for Shelby.

Fully two thirds of the twenty-six cars built that year remain unaccounted for. Again, the field is wide open for fakes, but it's also wide open for legitimate finds. And once again, the SAAC has, locked away, paperwork that can help a prospective buyer unravel the mystery and determine if a particular car is genuine.

1968

The SCCA turned the heat up even higher for the next year's Trans-Am. A-Sedan rules were softened a bit, allowing most notably for wider wheels and flares and a maximum engine size of 305ci *regardless* of original displacement. That meant Ford could punch out the 289 to take full advantage of the rules. That seemed, at least, to be a big advantage.

By pushing the stroke 0.125in, the engine displacement was brought up to 302ci. The block was strengthened to cover the added strain, but the real work was done on the heads. They were developed with information from the NASCAR 427 program, which Shelby had tapped (to great effect) for the 427 Cobra. The new heads featured straight-through intake ports with the pushrods right in the airflow (so-called tunnel-port heads). Previously the ports had to wind around the rods and lost some efficiency. The new heads also allowed for larger valves, and the whole assembly was much more amenable to porting and polishing than the old setup.

Built and developed by Ford instead of Shelby, the 302 had more than 440hp but diddley-squat for reliability. The tunnel-port drank oil like Dean Martin downed martinis, and when it inevitably starved out, the results were predictable. During the year, Shelby's engines were changed like dirty underwear.

Meanwhile, the Camaro had been honed even finer and Mark Donohue led the Trans-Am going away. Only at the earliest races, and when the Penske team suffered an unusual problem, did the Mustangs win. There's only one place you can go from the top, and in 1968 Ford went that way; it was a frustrating year.

Because their 1968 cars were so similar to the 1967 ones—the only changes were those that any team could easily have performed—Shelby decided not to make any customer cars for the year. To maintain a two-car team at each race, Shelby prepared five new 1968 racers and updated two of the 1967 cars as back-ups. (As it turned out, the older cars never saw a starting grid.) As things turned out, Shelby was wise not to sell replicas in any case—it's doubtful many racers would have been interested after seeing the troubles Ford's own team was having. Only two of the 1968 Trans-Am Shelbys are currently accounted for, one of them a leftover 1967 car that never raced in 1968 form.

1969

After the troubles of 1968, Ford decided that they had better rethink this notion of insisting on tunnel-port 302s in their racing cars. In the fall of 1968, Shelby and Ford did extensive studies on three possible 1969 powerplants, and were determined to choose and develop one of them based on realistic test results, instead of what had looked good on paper in the engineering lab.

The engines were the aluminum-head Gurney-Eagle 302, the old tunnel-port, and a new canted-valve 302 that would come to be called the Boss. The Gurney-Eagle was fastest, the Boss 302 came in behind it, and the tunnel-port trailed in last place—which was just as well, since nobody wanted to use the dreaded thing anyway.

Unfortunately, the exotic aluminum heads of the Gurney-Eagle ruled it out of the contest. Trans-Am rules stated that 1,000 copies of an engine had to be built to homologate it for competition, and there was no way Ford would build, let alone warranty, 1,000 motors like that. That left the Boss 302, and the tunnel-port engine was unceremoniously dumped by the wayside.

Ford constructed two 428 Cobra Jet-style fastback Mustang Mach 1s as their prototype 1969 Trans-Am cars, and shipped them to Kar Kraft for preparation. From there, one car went to Shelby and the other to Bud Moore, where they were stripped again and *really* prepared for competition. With the needed specifications in hand, Shelby received three plain-vanilla 1969 Mustang fastbacks and began turning them into race cars. They were lightened considerably—by 1969, Ford's pony was looking more like a twelve-hand Clydesdale—and the rest of the weight was redistributed to come up with a 50:50 balance front to rear. Roll cages were put in, and following the more lenient 1969 rules, the interiors were stripped out, the windows were replaced with lightweight units suspended on fabricated tracks and rollers, and an extensive rebuild of the suspension system ensued. Koni shocks, stiff springs, honking big antiroll bars, override traction bars (when Shelby gets an idea in his head there's no shifting it), disc brakes, and a Watts linkage to locate the rear end were all installed.

Ford again constructed the engines that Shelby and Moore would use, but this time the results were more successful. A pair of Holley carbs capable of 1,235cfm *each* were mounted atop the new Boss engines, monstrous valves and a radical cam lived inside, and gigantic tubular headers scavenged the combustion chambers. In the end, Ford's own people wrangled 470 pretty trusty horses out of the 5.0liter V-8; a considerable gain from the 289s of just two years earlier.

For all of its efforts, Trans-Am got tougher in kind. Factory teams from Chevrolet (Camaro), AMC (Javelin), Pontiac (Firebird), and the opposing Bud Moore-Ford camp went up against Shelby, and the results—while more encouraging than the year before—still came up short. The Penske-Donohue combo proved too tough once more, and they took their second title while Shelby managed only one first-place finish and a lot of DNFs.

At season's end, Ford announced it was cutting back its racing operations. Publicly it claimed it had already proven its point, but privately it saw that larger and larger sums of money seemed to be bringing smaller and smaller results. A minimum of research and development money to Cosworth's Formula 1 engine program was now buying more good press than whole shovelfuls of Trans-Am dough could provide.

Bud Moore got the nod as Ford's only factory team for 1970, and Shelby decided to git while the gittin' was good. Adding two Trans-Am championships to his trophy case was enough; it was time to move on.

As in 1968, Shelby didn't build any customer cars in 1969. Just five 1969 Shelby-built Trans-Am fastbacks appeared, and one was written off completely after Horst Kwech had a terrible crash at the Michigan International Speedway season opener. The other four have disappeared.

When Is a Shelby *Not* a Shelby?

In answer to the question posed in the chapter title, more often than you'd think. Cobras have the good or bad fortune of being so valuable that a total wreck is simply impossible. A finished, legitimate Cobra will always be worth enough money to justify whatever repairs it might need.

That's good for the Cobra fancier, but it also creates a serious problem. The SAAC calls them "air cars," and it's a good name—these are cars that have been conjured up out of thin air and then passed off as the real McCoy. It's not uncommon for two or more Cobras to exist, all claiming the same serial number. This usually happens when a car was balled up long ago and its various bits were sold off. Later, when Cobras became more valuable than anyone could have expected, three cars might have been rebuilt from the pieces of one, with the owner of the frame tubes constructing one, the holder of the title constructing another, and perhaps someone with nothing more than a photocopy of the registration and a steering wheel making the third.

So who actually owns the real Cobra? And what about the value of the other two cars? Obviously, the third example is an out and out fake. *If* (and it's a big if) this car was *excellently* prepared, it might be as thrilling to drive as any other Cobra. It is nevertheless *not* a Cobra, however, and its value will suffer accordingly. (It's possible that such a car may be fun to drive and available at a bargain-basement price. At the same time, complete fakes can be troublesome and downright dangerous at speed. Who knows how skilled the assembler was?)

So an air car won't bring anything like the money a real Cobra would, right? Normally yes, but only *if* (and this is a really big if) no other Cobra surfaces with the same serial number. Otherwise, no one may ever be the wiser—the car could be perceived and accepted as a legitimate Cobra brought back from the dead.

This is something the SAAC goes to great lengths to prevent, and anyone intentionally faking a Cobra runs the very real risk of being found out. Should the car have passed unwittingly on to another owner, however, that owner is the one who's going to get burned—and that, in a nutshell, is the thing to watch out for with Cobras. Since Cobras go for huge sums of money today, if the legitimate guts and paperwork haven't been sunk in New York's East River, it's likely to surface sooner or later—with expensive results for the owner of the air car.

But now let's get back to those other two cars. Technically, the person with legal and rightful possession of the mainframe tubes is the only one who can legitimately claim to have a Cobra. The owner of the title owns nothing more than a sheet of paper—titles are too easy to come by for it to mean anything else without the frame, the heart of the car.

As you can imagine, the various permutations of situations like this lead into some very gray areas. The best advice of all is to simply stay away from anything that sounds either too fishy or too good to be true. The SAAC ought to be able to verify or dismiss most owners' claims without too much trouble, but of course any Cobra faker has access to the same information that you do. Eye "history unknown" cars with a good deal of suspicion, size up the seller well, and stick to known quantities if you've got a choice.

The fear that someone will try to pass a kit car off as a real Cobra isn't very realistic. All the kits built in an organized fashion differ from legitimate Cobras in a tremendous number of ways, least of all not having proper ID plates and papers. After reading this book and inspecting the photos, a kit should be readily apparent to you—in truth, it's a pretty dumb seller who would even try this ruse, and it takes an even dumber buyer to fall for it.

Fake Shelby Mustangs, on the other hand, can be a lot harder to detect. Sometimes even a real expert will be hard pressed to tell a rebodied car—a standard Mustang that's been given the parts and title of a (presumably crashed or rusted beyond repair) legitimate Shelby—from the real thing. More common than a rebody, though, is a plain-Jane Mustang that gets Shelby-ized by an owner who wants but can't afford the real thing.

It's certainly possible to stick absolutely every part onto a stock Mustang that Shelby American did, and while the result may look like a Shelby, walk like a Shelby, and talk like a Shelby, in the eyes of investors it's *not* a Shelby. Shelbys are valuable not just for what they can do, but for their history.

Keep a sharp eye out for equipment that doesn't seem to jibe with what a Shelby should have. Look out for shaky paper trails at the DMV, and for ID plates that either don't match the car's engine numbers, don't indicate the equipment found on the car, or don't show it to be a real Shelby in any way. The easiest things to spot are engine and plant codes that don't read the way they ought to.

All prospective Shelby Mustang buyers should consider using the *Mustang Plate Decoder Book* (available from Classic Motorbooks), an exhaustive and inexpensive data source which covers all 1964½-1973 Mustang VIN codes and ID tag locations.

Shelby American Automobile Club

Most of the definitive information we have today on actual Shelby hardware results from the efforts of the Shelby American Automobile Club (SAAC), which has spent most of the time since Shelby American ceased production making some order out of what Shelby wrought. Many of the familiar terms we use today are actually classifications the SAAC came up with to identify certain vehicles. An FIA Cobra, for example, means something very specific today—but that term was actually coined after the fact to denote a certain run of cars that Shelby American and AC merely produced as needed.

This book adheres to, and relies on, a great deal of SAAC information and terminology. The club has taken a mind-boggling amount of information and processed it, verified it, and compiled it in a wholly professional manner; much of what we know about these cars is a by-product of their hard work and enthusiasm. To get inside advice from the experts on any Shelby-Ford product, join the club before you buy; it's probably the best investment you can make in this market.

(The SAAC can be contacted at Box 788, Sharon, Connecticut 06069.)

One particularly valuable thing the SAAC has done is to assemble the *Shelby American World Registry* which is updated and reprinted approximately every five years, available from Classic Motorbooks and the SAAC itself. The *Registry* gives a concise sketch of the individual history—often including original specifications, previous owners and competition activities if any—of as many cars as the SAAC has been able to catalog and document. Virtually all of the historically important Shelbys are outlined, and a staggering number of street models are included as well. A quick look in the *Registry* can often answer—or raise—all the most important questions about a particular Shelby's history and legitimacy.

Still, the SAAC is the first to admit that the Shelby story remains unfinished. There will forever be one more puzzle to solve and one more surprise popping up; that's a big part of the fun. I heartily encourage you to contact me through Classic Motorbooks as you discover these mysteries, or write the SAAC.

Cobra Kits and Replicas

The Cobra is the most copied automobile in the world, bar none. At any given time since 1985 there have been more than a dozen Cobra replica builders around, all in varying states of financial health and creating a varying quality of car.

The general sense one gets when discussing Cobra replicas is that the market offers a few excellent choices and quite a few more poor excuses. Some builders like England's Autokraft and America's ERA Replica Automobiles, Everett-Morrison, and Contemporary—there are a few others as well—have put out such consistently good products that the machines are offered grudging respect even by owners of the original breed. Occa-

Rather different from the way real Cobras look under the skin, most replicas of reasonable quality offer one substantial improvement over the original: hefty side-impact crash bars. *Nick Nicaise*

Most Cobra kits get the full S/C treatment with roll bar, Le Mans stripes, and the whole nine yards. It makes sense—as long as you're starting from scratch, you might as well go all the way. *Nick Nicaise*

sionally a replica comes along that surpasses the original in many respects, most notably in driver safety. More often, however, the product is little more than a Cobra-like body tossed over a cobbled-up frame.

Suspensions range from meticulous recreations of the original to a complete hash of Pinto and Chevette pieces. MGB and Datsun Z-car steering racks are often used in conjunction with Jaguar E-Type rear ends and suspensions. Engines run the gamut from full-race 427 Fords to small-block Chevrolets to Range Rover V-8s and Mustang II four-bangers. Bodies range from exact recreations in aluminum to fiberglass hulls that only marginally recreate the lines of AC's roadster.

The only replica builder thus far to have gained any real claim to the AC name is Autokraft, a small firm run out of the industrial park that has sprouted up on the infield of England's old Brooklands circuit. Auto-kraft began as a repair garage for AC cars, grew into a restoration shop, a parts supplier and manufacturer, and finally the owners of numerous AC tools and the right to use the AC name. Aluminum bodies—nearly every other Cobra replica is made of fiberglass—are hammered out on AC's original bucks. The chassis is virtually identical to an original Cobra's except where changes had to be made to accommodate safety regulations and the car's slightly larger cockpit. Autokraft and Ford entered into a handshake agreement whereby Ford supplied DOT (Department of Transportation) approved engines and Autokraft utilized Ford dealer networks for their US sales. The project has been scaled back considerably since the early days, but AC Mark IVs, as they're called, can still be obtained new for a price.

In the United States, companies like Shell Valley and Unique Motorcars are making inroads into the market by offering quality kits and turn-key vehicles, but the most famous makers are still probably ERA and Everett-Morrison, two builders dating back a spell. (ERA has also turned its attention to a marvelous recreation of the GT40.)

Cobra replicas and kits can offer a legitimate alternative to the Shelby fan who either doesn't have the money or the desire to drive a Cobra on the road. (A number of Cobra owners, dismayed at the thought of risking their quarter-million-dollar cars on the street, have also gotten their mitts on a replica to drive around.) On the other hand, a good Cobra replica can be alarmingly expensive and a poor Cobra replica can be one awfully lousy car. There are tomes and tomes out there written about kit cars, including a number of helpful catalogs, to help you make a wise decision if you want to go this route. You would be well advised to spend a lot of time hitting the books before ever leaving your living room.

A set of replica Sunburst (Halibrands are also available) wheels are one of the more expensive pieces of a kit, but they're almost a necessity if anyone's to be fooled. *Nick Nicaise*

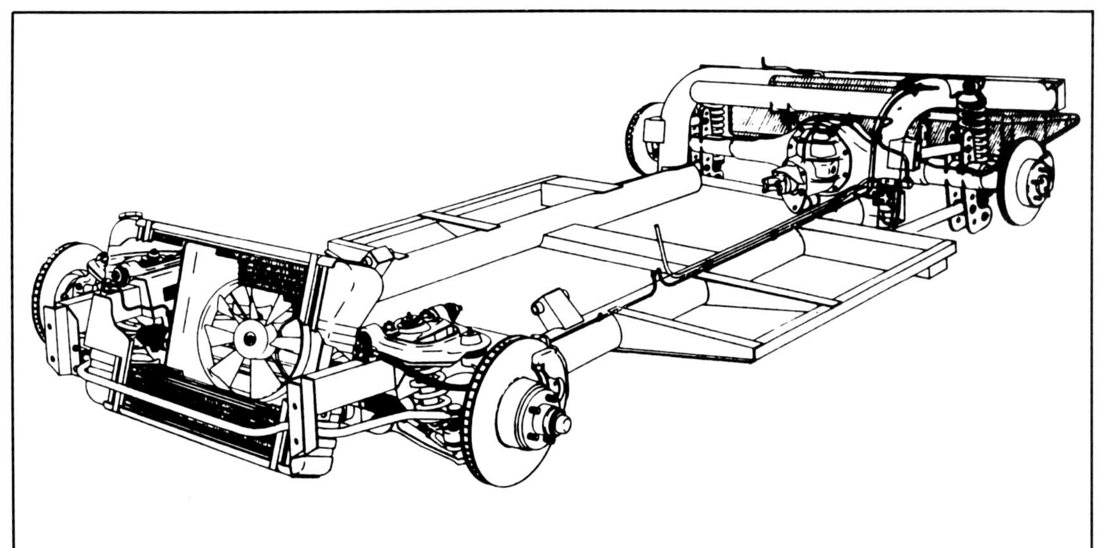

Under the skin, an Everett-Morrison 427 Replica chassis is robust, rigid, and well-engineered. It's not, however, a whole lot like the original Cobra, as evidenced by the live Ford rear axle and Mustang II front suspension. Replicas are just plain *not* Cobras—but judging from their sales figures, many people don't mind. *Everett-Morrison*

Shelby/Ford Production Numbers and VINs

Leaf-Spring Cobra

260 Cobra	75
289 Cobra	574
Daytona coupe	6
Total	655

Leaf-Spring Cobra VIN
CSX2–
COB60–
COX60–

King Cobra

King Cobra, Shelby factory racer	5
King Cobra, privateer	3
Total	8

King Cobra VIN

CM/1/63	CM/1/64
CM/3/63	CM/4/64
CM/5/63	CM/5/64
CM/6/63	CM/6/64

Coil-Spring Cobra

427 Cobra chassis only	3
427 Type 65 Super Coupe	1
427 Cobra, street	292
427 Cobra, competition	21
427 S/C	31
Total	348

Coil-Spring Cobra VIN
CSX3–
COB61–
COX61–

1965 Shelby

1965 GT350, street	516
1965 GT350, competition and drag cars	46
Total	562

1965 Shelby VIN
SFMR–
SFMS–
1965 Ford VIN
5R09K–

1966 Shelby

1966 GT350, general production	1,374
1966 GT350, Hertz	1,000
1966 GT350 convertible, not for public sale	6
Total	2,380

1966 Shelby VIN
SFMS–
1966 Ford VIN
5R09K– (cars 001-252)
6R09K– (cars 253-2380)

1967 Shelby

1967 GT350	1,175
1967 GT500	2,048
1967 GT500, notchback prototype	1
1967 GT500, convertible prototype	1
Total	3,225

1967 Shelby VIN
67 + (engine code) + (transmission code) +
    (base component) + F + (color code) +
    (interior code) + (five-digit production
    number)

Codes
Engine: 2 = 289, 4 = 428
Transmission: 0 = manual, 1 = automatic
Base: 1 = a/c, 2 = thermoactor, 3 = a/c and thermoactor
Color: 1 = bronze, 2 = dark blue, 3 = black, 4 = white, 5 = dark green, 6 = gray metallic, 7 = lime green, 8 = Brittany Blue, 9 = red, 0 = Acapulco Blue
1967 Ford VIN
7R02K– (289)
7R02Q– (428)

1968 Shelby

1968 GT350, fastback	1,253
1968 GT350, convertible	404
1968 GT500, fastback	1,140
1968 GT500, convertible	402
1968 GT500KR, fastback	933
1968 GT500KR, convertible	318
Total	4,450

1968 Shelby VIN
8T + (body code) + (engine code) + (six-digit Ford production number) + (five-digit Shelby production number)
Codes
Body: 02 = fastback, 03 = convertible
Engine: J = 302, S = 428, R = 428 Cobra Jet
1968 Ford VIN (below Shelby ID plate and on driver's door) First eleven characters of Shelby VIN plus additional information.
Additional information includes:
Color: A = black, I = lime green, M = white, Q = medium blue, R = dark green, T = red, W = yellow, X = dark blue, Y = gold
Transmission: 5 = manual, W = C–4, U = C–6

1969-1970 Shelby

1969–1970 GT350, fastback	1,085
1969–1970 GT350, convertible	194
1969–1970 GT500, fastback	1,536
1969–1970 GT500, convertible	335
Total	3,153*

*The most expert estimates indicate 789 vehicles produced as 1970 models. All 1969 and 1970 Shelby numbers are approximate; production may be slightly higher.
1969 Shelby VIN
(Year code) + F + (body code) + (engine code) + 48 + (four-digit production number)
Codes
Year: 9 = 1969, 0 = 1980
Body: 02 = fastback, 03 = convertible
Engine: M = 351, R – 428

Index